PRAISE FOR PILGRIM SPOKES

"Neil Hanson takes you on a journey that's both on the road and in the mind. For him, travel sparks observations on a myriad of topics, which he shares in his sparkling prose."

—**Stan Purdum,** author of *Roll Around Heaven All Day* and *Playing in Traffic*

"*Pilgrim Spokes* delivers a delightful blend of travelogue, cycling insights, and reflections. . . . [It's] a vivid read filled with personal reflection, philosophical insights, physical challenges, and a dose of spirituality that immerses the reader in an exhilarating ride."

—**D. Donovan,** Senior Reviewer, *Midwest Book Review*

"The clear and engaging voice, the conversations, and the introspection makes *Pilgrim Spokes* much more than just a journal of biking across the country. It's also entertaining and informative."

—**Jim Hoy,** author of *Flint Hills Cowboys*

"Hanson is a thoughtful narrator. . . Readers will consequently feel fortunate to find themselves immersed in meditations. . . this isn't just a book for bicycle enthusiasts; it's also for any fan of the examined life."

—**Kirkus Reviews**

BOOKS BY NEIL M. HANSON

CYCLING REFLECTIONS

Pilgrim Wheels (2015)
Pilgrim Spokes (2016)
Pilgriming the Trace (scheduled for 2017)

OTHER CYCLING BOOKS

The Pilgrim Way (2015)

NON-CYCLING BOOKS

Peace at the Edge of Uncertainty (2010)

Additional information on Neil's books can be found on page 271.

PILGRIM SPOKES

PILGRIM SPOKES

CYCLING EAST ACROSS AMERICA
NEIL M. HANSON

MEDICINE LODGE, KS

HIGH PRAIRIE PRESS DENVER

ANNAPOLIS, MD

HIGH PRAIRIE PRESS
6403 South Hudson Street
Centennial, CO 80121
www.highprairiepress.com
HighPrairiePress@gmail.com

Printed in the United States of America

First Printing, 2016

ISBN: 978-1-944868-01-7

Library of Congress Control Number: 2016903621

Speaking engagements and other author events scheduled through:
High Prairie Press
Neil M. Hanson
neilhansonauthor@gmail.com

Grateful acknowledgment is made to Jim Hoy for permission to reprint material from *Flint Hills Cowboys*.

Editing by Erin Willard, www.erincopyeditor.com

Book design and illustrations by K. M. Weber, www.ilibribookdesign.com

I thought of that while riding my bike.

Albert Einstein, on the theory of relativity

For Christine

CONTENTS

INTRODUCTION

*Traveling leaves you speechless, then
turns you into a storyteller.*

Ibn Battuta

Pilgrim Spokes is the second of two books that tell the story
of a journey I took across America by bicycle as I approached
the age of 60. The first book in the series is *Pilgrim Wheels*,
which is woven around the western half of the journey, from
Monterey in California to Medicine Lodge in Kansas. This
book—*Pilgrim Spokes*—begins at Medicine Lodge and conveys
the reader along the eastern half of the journey to Annapolis
on the east coast.

I averaged about 100 miles a day as I rode, so the trip
took a little over a month. My work prevented me from taking
the time off to make the entire trip in a single season, so you'll
notice a transition of time that occurs early in the book, while
I'm still in Kansas. Something else that changes during the ride
is the company I keep. For about half the journey I rode by
myself, and about half the time I rode with my friend Dave.

It's one journey, so why two books? A simple answer
would be nice, but I don't think one fits here. The complete

answer revolves around things like taking the time for deep and meaningful reflection, transforming the pace of a bicycle ride into a book, and wanting to tell a more complete story.

First, the time thing. Time for reflection was one of the many gifts I discovered on my pilgrimage across America. Reflection on myself, the places I rode through, the people I met, the things I discovered. My sojourn wasn't about the million-and-a-half pedal strokes it took me to get from one coast to the other, or about the route I took, or about the places I slept at night. It was a wonderful adventure of discovery, and I want the story I share with readers to expose as much of that discovery as possible. I want my reflections to be deep enough for the reader to see the real journey, not just the lines on a map.

Then there's the pace. Touring on a bicycle brings a different pace to the wandering. Clipping along at 14 mph let me spend a whole lot more time in each of the 3400 miles I found between the Pacific and the Atlantic. On a 777, the trip from coast to coast happens in the time required for a nice long nap—a magazine article version of the trip. In a car, it's a real passage that lasts several days—an entire book, maybe. But on a bicycle, this is a pilgrimage. Trying to smash all that story into a single book feels like a disservice to both the odyssey and to the reader of the story. Sharing this journey in two books brings the right pace into the story.

And finally, there are the people who became part of the journey. Their stories, and how those stories resonated within me, are something that deserve telling. A beautiful Martin guitar sang to me from the corner of an old house in Missouri. I held it for a few minutes, coaxed a little music from it, and learned a lot about myself from the fella who owned that guitar. I became the steward of the story of the conversation we had, and failing to share that story in a way that does it justice, would feel to me like cheating.

For these reasons and more, I've told this story in two volumes. Is it absolutely necessary to read volume one before volume two? Probably not. But honestly, I think it'll make for a more rich understanding of the journey if you do.

Pilgrim Wheels and *Pilgrim Spokes* are journey stories, not logistics guides. Cyclists will love them, but so will anyone who loves a good journey story. For folks who want logistics details of the trip, I have a little companion book about those specifics that I love to share. It's packed with the particulars that bike nerds like me love, including details of the route I took, the gear I carried, minimalism as a touring style, training, the cycling equipment I carried, provisioning, and much more. It's called *The Pilgrim Way*, and it's all about those logistical things that *Pilgrim Wheels* and *Pilgrim Spokes* aren't about. If you're interested in a copy, get in touch with me, or you can get it through any of the normal bookseller channels.

Happy reading to you. I hope you enjoy the stories I share about the journey as much as I enjoy sharing them.

It would not be at all strange if history came to the conclusion that the perfection of the bicycle was the greatest incident in the nineteenth century.

Detroit Tribune, late 1800s

PROLOGUE

*Wandering re-established the original harmony
which once existed between man and universe.*

Anatole France

Medicine Lodge seems a perfect stopping point for this story. Rolling into the humid farmland east of Medicine Lodge, the texture of the places ahead of us would clearly be different from what was behind us. The ride continued, and the ride through the eastern half of the country becomes the next story. It's co-incidence that Medicine Lodge is at the halfway point in terms of miles, since the real division of story comes from the change in the character of the land and the ride that happens there.

The sweetness of that morning ride into Medicine Lodge is something I remember well as I type these words—an exclamation point to a journey that was packed with sweet moments and lush memories, along with a little pain now and again. Writing about these memories and moments nourishes my anticipation for writing the rest of the story, the story of the completion of the ride to Annapolis.

Originally published as the Epilogue at the end of *Pilgrim Wheels*.

Anticipation. Such a lonely word any more. In our quest for instant gratification, we sometimes lose touch with the sweetness of anticipation. We think longing is a bad thing, that longing implies we don't have something we want. When we instantly get the thing we think we want, we can't figure out why having it feels so hollow. It's the longing we miss. The anticipation. The flirting.

Telling the story of yesterday helps us define the palette for our next adventure. It's how we learn to flirt with tomorrow. And in the flirting, we discover the true gift in the story we tell.

KANSAS

MEDICINE LODGE, KS

I was born upon the prairie, where the wind blew free, and there was nothing to break the light of the sun. I was born where there were no enclosures, and where everything drew a free breath.

The great Comanche war chief, Ten Bears

COTTONWOOD FALLS, KS

HOGS AND SPANDEX

*I find that the great thing in this world is not so much
where we stand as in what direction we are moving:
To reach the port of heaven, we must sail sometimes
with the wind and sometimes against it— but we must
sail, and not drift, nor lie at anchor.*

Oliver Wendell Holmes

DAY 20 • MEDICINE LODGE TO WELLINGTON, KANSAS

If food can be spiritual, then chicken fried steak belongs somewhere up on the altar. Plenty of salt in the breading, just a
little spicy, a big pile of potatoes spilling over it, a blanket of
sausage gravy, a couple of eggs crowded onto the plate, some
bacon on the side just to fill in the edges . . .
Does better food exist?

Dave and I are enjoying breakfast at a truck stop diner
in Medicine Lodge, Kansas, and I know I'm not alone in my
culinary opinion, because at the table next to us is a big truck
driver enjoying his massive plate of chicken fried steak with
gusto. A napkin tucked into the top of his shirt, fork firmly
gripped in his right hand and knife in his left, there's a rhythm

to the methodical assault he's making on the haute cuisine à la Midwest that sits on the table in front of him.

Dave gets up and heads toward the restroom as I notice a couple of guys in a booth close to us are chuckling, looking our way occasionally. One of them is pretty burly, and the other is lean. Both are heavily tattooed and dressed in the unmistakable uniform of Harley riders out on the road for some fun.

Dave and I, in contrast, are decked out in our most intimidating spandex shorts. We toughen the look up a bit with brightly colored cycling jerseys for maximum visibility and nerd factor, adding wobbly cycling shoes to help us strut with real intimidation while walking, our cleats clicking on the hard floor like tap shoes.

I catch the lean fella's eye the next time he looks over at me, giving him a nod and a smile, acknowledging the fun they're having. He nods back and asks, "Where you fellas ridin' to this mornin'?

"We're not for sure yet. At least Wellington, maybe Winfield if the heat or wind doesn't get too bad."

Burly Fella raises his eyebrows, straightens his neck, then cocks his head slightly in a way that says something like, *"Holy smokes that's a lotta ridin'."* He still hasn't made eye contact with me, apparently not sure yet if it's okay to be conversing with these weird bicycle nerds.

Lean Fella is clearly the communicator of the two, and continues the dialogue. "Man alive, that's gotta be 75 or 100 miles, right? You guys just now startin' out for the day?"

"Yeah, Wellington's probably another 70 or 75 miles, Winfield another 20 or 25 after that. But no, we started back in Coldwater this morning, about 40 miles west of here."

"Wait a minute. You tellin' me you've already ridden your little bicycle 40 miles this morning, and you're gonna ride another 70 or more? That's like 100 miles, right?"

I nod slowly, not sure whether to update his math for accuracy, or just let it slide in the interest of friendly diplomacy.

In the end, I opt for accuracy. "Yeah actually it'll be at least 110 miles, depending on whether we stop in Wellington."

He doesn't take any offense. Instead, the two look at each other for a minute, recalibrating their interaction with us. I get the clear impression they're pushing away from me a little bit, and I'm wondering if it's because they figure we're a little crazy, or maybe they've reconsidered us and now think we might be tough guys who shouldn't be fooled with since we can ride our bicycles so far.

There's a third possibility, which I don't consider, but it makes itself plain as Dave returns and sits down.

Lean Fella addresses Dave with a tone that makes it clear he's about to show me up and expose my exaggerations of how far we're going to ride. "Hey, how many miles you guys gonna ride those bicycles today?"

Dave looks up toward the ceiling, for just an instant, calibrating what he thinks the miles will be. "We hope to make it to Winfield, which will be 135 miles. But we're learning not to set our expectations too high—the wind hasn't been real friendly to us so far. We might end up stopping at Wellington, which would only be 114 or 115 miles."

Lean Fella sits back in the booth, sails deflated. Dave looks at me with a question in his eye, wondering how this conversation got started up with these guys. Not the interaction you'd expect in this small-town diner—a couple of tough biker types joking with the old geezers in tight spandex shorts.

Humans are funny animals. We think we're special in the whole scheme of the food pyramid, that we're in control of our actions, and that we're all such unique individuals. We think we're making decisions about how we behave. But in the end, here in a small-town diner on a hot July morning in western Kansas, we're just some big apes pounding our chests a bit and struttin' around, sizing each other up, intent on seeing who claims the alpha spot, everyone wanting to avoid injury and bloodshed if possible.

In our case, struttin' involves a few words, careful verbal jabs back and forth, accompanied by the timeless body language that all males in my ape species seem to use. No blood is shed, and a hierarchy is established within a few short minutes. I admit I never know what the hierarchy is—only that it got established somehow. We walk out the front door together, trading light-hearted banter.

The pavement outside radiates the scalding heat of a cloudless summer day. It's mid-morning, and already the hot air wraps me in the sense that I've stepped into an oven. Dave and I grab our bicycles as we walk past, and continue with the bikers out onto the sea of blistering pavement.

Our newfound buddies are fellow vagabonds on the road, packs tied on the back of their big Harleys, *Easy Rider*-style. As has been the case with motorcyclists all across the western half of the country, we establish a bond quickly with these fellow two-wheeled adventurers, trading brief stories of the road behind and hopes and plans for the road ahead. Burly Fella is still a little unsure about how wise it is to fraternize with gaily clad bicyclists, but he participates in the rituals.

Dave and I saddle up and start pedaling east along US 160 while our two new friends idle their big machines over to the gas pumps to spend some more money. We're a couple of miles out of town by the time they pass us on their big hogs. Lean Fella slows down to ride beside me for a few minutes, matching my measly 15 mph pace. We continue the good-natured banter we established back at the diner, cementing our bond as allies on the road. Finally, he decides it's time to catch up with his buddy.

"Hey, you guys be careful out here on the road," he says with a serious look of friendship on his face.

"We will for sure," I reply. "You guys do the same. And hey, leave a little chicken fried steak for us up at the next diner, okay?"

With a deep and good-hearted laugh, he extends his right hand to me and we bump knuckles awkwardly, then he drops his hand back to the throttle and takes off up the road, lifting his left hand high in salute as he passes Dave up ahead of me. Dave. Mr. Consistency. Mr. Focus. He barely notices as Lean Fella passes him. He's busy calculating a new average speed so far in the day, or maybe vectoring in on exactly what time we'll arrive in Wellington, or maybe whether we'll be able to make it all the way to Winfield today. This has become our pattern out on the road—Dave establishing the pace, maintaining the statistical dashboard for the day's ride, continuously aware of possible final destinations for the day, and what time we're likely to get there.

And me, perpetually trying to keep up with Dave, but gawking at every marsh hawk that glides across the fence line, stopping to take pictures far more often than is really necessary, blissfully unaware of our progress or pace for the day. Dave, good friend that he is, tolerates my daydreaming pace and overly romantic perspective, stopping occasionally to wait for me to catch up. We're another 10 miles or so up the road when I see him pulled over waiting for me on the side of the road, finishing off one of his water bottles. He pretends he wanted to stop anyway to get a drink, and I pretend to believe him.

"We're making really good time this morning," he informs me. I'm positive that he knows exactly what our average speed has been, though he meets me at our middle ground with his statement that's accurate though not too precise.

"We are—that crosswind that's come up from the south doesn't seem to be slowing us down much."

Dave looks off to the south, as if the wind were visible in some way. And actually, several times during our crossing of Kansas, the wind has been quite visible in the form of boiling dust clouds or flags nearly ripped from flagpoles. But so far today the wind is light, and not in our face enough to have an appreciable impact. "Yeah. Unless it hits us hard or something else slows us down, it's really possible we could make it to Winfield today."

"Cool. Let's hope you haven't pissed off the wind gods

again, and we can finally get a day of respite from the southern blast furnace."

Dave smiles, replacing his empty water bottle onto his frame. "I'm going through water pretty fast. I hope there's a decent place to fill our bottles at our next stop. I think there's a town in another 10 miles or so."

Sure enough, 10 miles further up the road brings us into the little burg of Attica. I know my schoolteachers from back in the sixties would love it if the name "Attica" brought to my mind the famous region in Greece, but instead my first thought is of the prison riots back in the early seventies. Once again, the obsession the media has with violence washes away the efforts of countless well-intentioned schoolteachers.

We find some shade where we relax and enjoy granola bars and cold water after filling our water bottles at the local convenience store. The landscape around us has changed significantly today, having crossed a very stark line from the west to the east. We rode down into Medicine Lodge this morning after a delightful ride through the Medicine Hills, a deeply beautiful place archetypical of the arid and desolate Great American West. Since leaving Medicine Lodge, the land has abruptly flattened out, our ribbon of road surrounded by tilled fields of corn and beans, the air around us markedly more humid. We've arrived in the more gentle farmland of the Midwest, and the eastern half of our journey across America has begun.

Gazing lazily out across the blistering July heat, I watch a peregrine falcon make a short but blazing-fast dive at a bird. Though I'm an amateur and mediocre birder at best, it seems to me unlikely that a peregrine would be this far east, but I'm also fairly confident that's what this is. I can't see for sure if it hits its prey, and I find myself wondering whether I'm rooting for the predator or the prey.

I don't have to think about it for long before realizing it's the falcon I'm rooting for. Sure I feel sympathy for the smaller prey, and don't want it to suffer, but there's no doubt in my mind as I chew on my granola bar. I'm rooting for the falcon today.

Leaving the shade, climbing back onto the bike and pedaling east, I realize that this morning the Kansas heat is the predator, and I'm the prey. I'm changing my vote—now I'm rooting for the prey.

FLIRTING WITH HEAT

No one will win the battle of the sexes,
there is too much flirting with the enemy.

Henry Kissinger

I figure we must be getting close to Wichita now, and I expect the manner and friendliness of the people will likely change for the worse. I'm pleasantly surprised to be wrong, and find that folks continue to be open and friendly, though traffic levels have picked up just a bit. Swinging out of the saddles, we lean our bikes against the big windows at a little sub shop in Harper.

"You doin' okay?" I ask Dave. "You look like you're hurtin' a bit."

"Boy this humidity—it's rough."

I look at the big sign above a bank across the street as we unbuckle our helmets and leave them on the bikes, feeling well-informed by the big bright "99F" that alternates with the current time of day on the sign.

"Yeah, this is the first blast of humidity we've really had to deal with, isn't it? I guess this is what we have to look forward to from now on."

Dave's face falls in recognition of this truth but is quickly transformed by a smile as we walk through the front door of the little place, and the blast of cool air conditioning bathes us in immediate respite from the heat. We stand motionless inside the door for a minute, basking in the cool reprieve from the oppressive furnace outside.

"You guys can just sit wherever you want." The cute waitress is looking at us like she's a bit concerned she'll need to call the medics if we don't sit down and rest.

We smile, and make our way to a booth along the window where we can keep an eye on the bikes outside. Not that we need to worry much about somebody taking them, because to do that they'd need to spend extra time outside, and put their bare hands on the hot metal of the bikes, not to mention having to do the work of either riding them off or loading them into a vehicle. Things that require work and produce warmth. Things I'm absolutely certain that nobody wants to do in the boiler that today has become.

"You sure you're okay, Dave? You look like the heat is taking it out of you."

"Yeah, I'm fine. I think this air conditioning will help a lot."

"It doesn't seem like you're taking in much water."

Dave picks up his water bottles from the table, realizing that one is still full. He reaches over and confirms that mine are empty. I emphasize my point: "I would have drunk more if I'd had it. I ran out five miles back down the road."

He looks off out the window, and I can see him thinking about this. I tease Dave often that he's a bit of a camel, taking in half the fluid I do when we ride. I imagine that his body probably just deals well with mild dehydration, but then when he gets into stressful heat like this, the low fluid levels make it harder for his body to deal effectively with the heat. It's unusual for Dave to be suffering more than I am on a ride. He's always in better shape than I am and is generally stronger, pound for pound. High heat is about the only condition that I endure better than he does.

"I need to drink more, that's all there is to it," he says with conviction.

On cue, the waitress comes over with a big pitcher of water, ready to fill our water glasses. I notice that she's really more than just cute—she's quite beautiful. As she reaches for a glass, I chime in.

"Actually, why don't you just leave the whole pitcher for us? When you come back to take our order, maybe bring a replacement. I'm pretty sure this one will be empty and we'll be ready for another."

She smiles the way women smile when they know they're good looking and know that their smile has a magical effect on men. We both smile back like goofballs, just like all men smile back at good-looking women who smile at them that way. She turns and walks away, aware that our eyes are following her. She turns a corner, and like puppets our eyes turn back to our conversation. We shake our heads in recognition of this pathetic male condition.

Dave says what we're both thinking. "Really, where do they learn that? Do they come out of the womb with some hidden little bit of knowledge that blossoms as they grow up? Is there a secret manual somewhere that's titled something like, *How to Use Your Complete Control Over Males to Your Greatest Advantage in Life'?*"

"Isn't there an old country and western song out there that says something about that?"

"Probably more than one!"

We both gaze out the window, contemplating the truth of the observation, languishing in the cool air as it saps the excess heat from our bodies. The waitress reappears with a full pitcher of water to replace the empty one on the table. We haven't even looked at the menu, but quickly glance at it and order something. Neither Dave nor I am a real connoisseur of food—eating is just a task to fill the tank. Most of the time it'd be easier if the waitress just brought out whatever she wanted and we'd eat it and be happy.

Our eyes follow the waitress once again as she walks away, and I wipe the remnants of the goofy smile from my face and say what we're both thinking. "Jeez. We're pathetically predictable creatures."

"Yeah, we're just a couple of harmless old men appreciating some beauty. I suppose this falls well over the line into objectifying her good looks though, doesn't it?"

"I guess so, but it's a ritual we all buy into. She smiles and moves to catch our attention, we give her our attention. At the end of the day she hopes for a bigger tip, and I suspect it usually works."

The shop is nearly empty, Dave and I the only real customers. Over against the far window a young man sits alone in a booth, and the waitress slides into the booth beside him while she waits for our order to come up. Obviously her boyfriend, he turns slightly and drapes his arm over the top of the booth behind her as she slides up against him. A happy young couple, clearly in love. Or something like that.

We both turn our attention back to our table, and Dave continues. "And in that case, it's about something more than a tip."

Chuckling, I answer, "Young love, right? Before they see the warts and foibles in one another."

"Yep. He's completely lost in her smile and all that other magic stuff she does. And she's . . . well who knows what women see in men, but she keeps that smile pointed at him, so she must see something."

"I've heard it said more than once that most of us build three big relationships in life. I guess the way I've really heard it is that we generally end up with three marriages in life."

Dave looks puzzled, and I continue. "Not necessarily three legal marriages and three legal divorces, though I'm sure it sometimes happens that way. But the notion, or at least my memory of it, is that first we have the passionate young love where we can't keep our hands off each other, then we evolve into the marriage where we build a family, and finally we need to find the marriage in which we can grow old together."

"I guess I can see that. Some couples can evolve through two or three of the marriages together, but some people end up with different partners in different marriages. Is that the idea?"

"Right, exactly. I suppose the fairytale version of the picture would show the same couple in all three relationships."

Dave turns his gaze back out the window, cogitating. "Yeah, I can definitely see that. Moving from the second to the third with the same person might be easier than moving from the first to the second."

"You think so? Why?"

"I don't know. I guess it seems like the first transition has so much working against it. It's founded and built completely on the kind of instinctive and chemical attraction that's steaming off those two in the booth across the way, instead of on any real knowledge of the other person. It's all chemistry, no intellect."

"Then once they have to start actually getting to know the person beneath all those hormones . . . Well, the odds just seem low, don't they?"

Dave nods in agreement. "And that second transition seems like it would have a better chance. The second marriage is going to last years or decades, and you're evolving together as people. If you can make the middle marriage work you can probably slide easily into the third one, right?"

I think about it for a while, pondering. "I don't know. Maybe. But in many ways that transition from the second phase to the third phase is just as big as the transition from the first phase to the second phase. I mean, just because I'm a good dad and provider doesn't mean I'm someone good to grow old with. Life changes completely when the kids are gone."

This is something I've thought about a lot, and Dave's intuition doesn't miss the depth of my comment. This is more than just a light and passing observation to me. Dave and I are both in that place in life where our kids are grown, and have fledged or are fledging. We've both been married for 25 or 30 years, and are both at this second transition point. I don't have any idea whether or not Dave and his wife have struggled with this transition or not, but I think my comments and demeanor give away that it's a significant passage I'm struggling with in my marriage.

The waitress sets our lunch on the table, along with another pitcher of water. We're quiet as we start into our subs. After a bite or two, Dave says, "You know, you might be right. Everything really does change when the kids leave, doesn't it?"

"It really does. Here you've spent the greatest part of your lives together as partners in raising children. That was your big purpose in life—taking care of your family. Then all of a sudden that's gone, and it's just the two of you looking across the table, wondering who the person on the other side of the table is."

"Yeah, I don't know if I'd agree with that. I mean, it's not like you haven't spent decades together. You ought to know each other."

"Sure, but you know the family partner, not the grow-old-together partner. Have you ever known somebody at work, and you only know them at work, where they wear a suit every day and have their work persona, and you know them well for years, then unexpectedly you run into them in a completely different setting, and you don't even recognize them?"

Dave thinks about it for a second, then smiles and nods in recognition of what I'm talking about. "Sure, and the more you know only the work persona of the individual, the harder it is to see them in the other context."

"Exactly!" I exclaim around a bite of sandwich. A little uncomfortable silence follows as we continue our lunch. Silence isn't unusual with Dave and me, but uncomfortable silence is. After a couple of bites, I try to move the conversation into more comfortable ground. "An interesting concept anyway; whether it holds water or not I can't say."

"Speaking of holding water, I'm making sure both these water bottles are filled to the brim when we leave here," Dave says as he packs his bottles with ice and pours icy water to the very lip.

Our waitress comes back with our check, and flashes one more of the magic smiles, eliciting once again the goofy grins from us that we're trying desperately not to display. When it's time to leave, we throw the cash onto the table, and Dave pauses while looking me in the eye. "So, in this case, did it work?"

"The flirting for the tip? I think it's about the same as we'd leave for any waitress who took good care of us."

"Hmmm. Yeah maybe." But clearly, he's not fully convinced.

"What was that country and western song lyric again?"

WHEN LIFE IS GOOD

*Grief can take care of itself; but to get the full value
of a joy you must have someone to divide it with.*
Mark Twain, *The Tragedy of Pudd'nhead Wilson*

Goofy grins are replaced by instant and copious sweat as we
wade back out into the muggy furnace. Ice in my water bottles
jingles enticingly in rhythm with the rocking of my bicycle as
I pedal down the road. It's a sweet sound on a hot day—ice
jostling in a water bottle. The serenade elicits pleasant emotions in the simple mix of thoughts and feelings that rock gently back and forth with me in the saddle of my bicycle rolling
through little Harper, Kansas.

   A simple pleasure. Subtle and quiet. Age has dramatically
improved my ability to savor simple pleasures. Thirty years
ago, my obsession with getting from point *A* to point *B* drove
wedges into more than one relationship in my life. My lack of
patience made me a far less thoughtful and pleasant person.

   On the whole, my list of warts and faults is probably longer today than it was thirty years ago. I've had decades to perfect my imperfections, after all. But all in all, I'm a lot happier

with the me I've become than with the me that age has left behind. A good deal of that happiness comes from my evolved ability to enjoy simple pleasures in their own time.

The rhythm of jostling ice comforts me as I drift through the quintessential rural farmland rolling past on either side of us. The roadside is dotted with picturesque farmsteads that look as though they were put there for Norman Rockwell to paint. The corn's healthy and tall, the wheat's been neatly cut, and the kitchen gardens are all trim and well-tended. The drivers give us the entire lane at nearly every opportunity. Folks are as friendly here as they've been all the way across Kansas.

Lumbering into Wellington, feeling the effects of the heat, we're a little intimidated by the bank of dark storm clouds in front of us, so we decide to take up our nightly temporary residence in a little hotel right along the highway. The air conditioning in the room roars and rattles like a freight train and still can't keep up with the heat.

"Our room seems to have a faulty air conditioner," I mention to the gal at the front desk as we head out to find some grub after showering up. I learn from her name tag that this is Betty.

"Probably not. None of them work well in this heat." Betty doesn't seem apologetic or concerned, just stating the facts. Dave and I look at each other, a bit at a loss.

"So do you suppose all of the motels in the area have this same problem—air conditioning systems that don't work in the summer?" My smart-ass tone is lost on Betty, as she looks around thoughtfully and cocks her head just a little bit, then answers.

"Might be. It's been pretty hot. But the thing is, if you wait until later when the sun is down, they cool pretty well."

A bit taken aback by the nonchalance of her attitude toward something that seems to me like a basic requirement for a motel room in Kansas in the depth of summer, it takes me a while to form an answer. "But the unit here in the lobby seems to be working fine—it's cool in here."

"Yeah this one seems to work well." An uncomfortable silence follows. Uncomfortable to me at least. Betty isn't bothered at all. A tiny shred of culpability in our situation finally seems to seep into her worldview, and she adds, "Hey I have a couple of fans; if you want you can borrow one for the room. But you have to turn it back in at the desk in the morning when you check out."

Hmmm. Good idea. The noise of a fan to drown out the incessant rattle of an air conditioning unit that's overtaxed. And so generous of her to offer. Dave is already headed toward the door, so I take the hint and follow him out into the heat. "So what do you think?" he says. "Do we want to try to find another hotel?"

"I don't know. I guess I'm lazy. I don't want to pack up and move. Besides, maybe she's right, maybe the room will cool down later."

Dave pokes his head back through the front door. "Hey we'll take you up on that fan. We'll pick it up on our way back to the room after supper."

When life is good—really good—it's hard for a bad situation to ruin it. I suppose it's a measure of how good life is right now that Dave and I both take our lodging situation in stride. The room never does cool down, and the air conditioning unit never shuts off all night. My sleep is fitful, and most likely filled with images of broken freight trains rattling across the hot and humid plains.

Still, life is good. Really good.

THE WINDS OF DECISION

Listen to the wind, it talks.
Listen to the silence, it speaks.
Listen to your heart, it knows.

Native American proverb

DAY 21 • WELLINGTON TO COTTONWOOD FALLS, KANSAS

We're in the saddle well before daybreak, headed east from Wellington. A dense cloud of mosquitos offers some resistance as we battle our way through it and into a convenience store to pick up morning calories to fuel us until we find a diner for breakfast. We consume the calories in the store, away from the insect horde outside, then run back outside and jump into our saddles so we can start moving down the road to try to escape the swarm. There's no thought of leisurely enjoyment of the morning air, as we're devoured by the vicious ferocity of the little winged creatures.

From the west coast to this point we've encountered no bugs to speak of, but here in Wellington we're reminded again that we've left the arid West, and are well into the humid Midwest.

Storms rolled through last night, leaving soppy ground and puddles along the side of the road. Fog lays in a dense blanket over our world this morning, creating a beautiful hush in the rare moments when cars aren't around us. Peaceful rural farmsteads peek out at us with soft edges, backlit by a warm sun working to burn through the mist. By the time we reach Winfield, the mist has been baked away by a sun promising to make itself felt all day.

The little town of Winfield feels healthy and quaint. Well-maintained and vibrant, it's clearly a regional center of commerce. Downtown is full of activity, and feels prosperous. We pull up to the Blues Cafe and step in for some breakfast.

It's clear that most everyone here knows one another. The waitress goes out of her way to share a few words with everyone. Our breakfast is delicious, and we enjoy the little snippets of conversation we're able to eavesdrop on as we fill our calorie tank for the rest of the morning. As I'm paying the check, the gal who apparently runs the place strikes up a conversation.

"Where you fellas riding today?"

"Well, in the long run, we're making our way across the country. Today, I think we'll feel good if we make it to Cottonwood Falls, and really good if we make it to Council Grove."

At this point, I've come to expect some exclamation of amazement at how far we're riding. But she never breaks stride for a second. I come to realize that this has been the case for most of our journey across Kansas—people just aren't as *taken* by the scope of our journey. I realize that here in the very heart of America, the truly conservative spirit of the backroads is evident in this lack of awe.

By conservative, I don't mean politically conservative. The political connotation of the word *conservative* reflects nothing at all of the true nature of conservatism. The media uses the word *conservative* to refer to folks who are right wing politically, which generally has nothing whatsoever to do with having a conservative outlook or a conservative nature.

In contrast, this rural American conservative spirit we've

been encountering across Kansas has to do with being concerned for the well-being of others without meddling in their business. It involves reaching out to help others without wanting recognition for the act. It's a quiet self-assurance that the world is generally a good place, and the best way to keep it that way is to be a good neighbor without asking for anything in return.

In the case of our breakfast hostess here in Winfield, Kansas, it means that she's interested in knowing about the ride, but isn't about to embarrass me by making a big deal about it. She's not going to ask too many questions but will gladly and attentively listen if I want to volunteer more information. Counting my change back to me, she displays the true caring spirit I'm coming to appreciate so much. "You fellas be careful out there today. The temperature's going above 100 every day, and the humidity is really bad. Do you have plenty of water? Lots of ice?"

"Yes ma'am, we've got plenty of water. Thanks for asking. We're getting better at dealing with the heat, but the humidity is the hard part, isn't it?"

She's looking me right in the eye like we've known each other our whole lives. She reaches across the counter and puts her hand lightly on my forearm, not really gripping, but enough touch to make sure she has my full attention. "That humidity will hurt you. You be careful out there." This woman has kept teenage boys out of trouble—that's clear from the weight carried by her tone and her look.

I smile and nod my thanks, pausing long enough to let her know I'm taking her seriously, before asking, "How is the traffic on 77 headed north?"

"The truck traffic is bad. But the shoulder is pretty good. You fellas stay on the shoulder when you ride, right?"

"Yep. We stay on the shoulder. Thanks for the good advice ma'am, and thanks for the great breakfast!"

Outside, sweat is already beaded on Dave's face. Winfield represents a real fork in the road for us, and I have no idea why we couldn't have talked about which fork to take when we were sitting in the air conditioning. Instead, we stand in some shade outside to discuss which route we want to take. If we continue east on 160, our route across the country will take a more southerly tack, through the Ozarks and south of the Mason-Dixon, ending up somewhere along the coastline of the Southeast. If we head north from here, we'll ride across the great midwestern farm country before arriving in the Appalachians and ending up around Annapolis.

Both routes sound good to us. The wild card is the Flint Hills, the heart of which we'll ride through if we cut north here. The region is the place I call home, as I spent my formative years there. It's one of the most beautiful places in America. I think Dave senses the draw inside me to ride through the Flint Hills, and makes it easy by suggesting we go north.

The fact that the wind out of the southeast is beginning to swirl up Main Street probably helps solidify our decision. We've been fighting the wind all the way across Kansas, and we're tired of the battle. Turning north here puts the wind at our back for the day. Decision made, we start pedaling north.

Big decisions are like that sometimes. A little emotional tug one way or the other, or maybe just the way the wind blows that day. A little tug, a puff of wind, and the course of the remainder of our journey is set.

THE MYTHOLOGY OF ME

"The land belongs to the future, Carl; that's the way it seems to me. How many of the names on the county clerk's plat will be there in fifty years? I might as well try to will the sunset over there to my brother's children. We come and go, but the land is always here. And the people who love it and understand it are the people who own it—for a little while."

Willa Cather, O Pioneers!

Decades ago, I rode my bike along this same route we'll be riding today. It was back in the seventies, and I was a dumb and reckless college kid. I'd been attending a bluegrass festival in Winfield and decided I wanted to ride my bike home to Manhattan. (Manhattan, Kansas, that is. We like to call it "The Little Apple.")

I have sweet memories of that ride. A slight south wind came up in the predawn hours and pushed me gently along as the sky in the east began to glow, blooming eventually into a beautiful blazing sunrise. Scissor-tailed flycatchers performed acrobatics in the growing light, and the sounds of birds filled the woods on either side of me. A chorus of frogs chimed in now and then, and crickets filled the lulls in the conversation of the universe unfolding around me.

Plus a few less-than-idyllic memories. An old bike, no lights, no helmet, no food, just a little water, and no money. Silly boy. Ignorance combined with a sense of invincibility must be one of the leading causes of disaster in the history of humans. Later in the day, a series of flat tires and a crippling headwind plagued me, and I ended up gratefully accepting a ride over the last 20 miles or so from a couple of college students.

As the miles north out of town roll beneath my tires, both memories of that day are rolling around in my brain. One idyllic, one tinged with some misery. But it's the idyllic memory that's at the forefront of my mind as Winfield fades behind us. I keep looking up the road, hoping to see that lonely highway, glimpse a few flycatchers, feel a wind at my back. We're taking it pretty easy and the shoulder is good here, so I ride beside Dave and tell him my story from long ago as we pedal along.

After finishing the story, I ask him, "Does it make me an eternal optimist that the half of the memory that's forefront in my mind right now is the half that includes a beautiful sunrise, a tailwind, and scissor-tailed flycatchers, instead of the miserable stuff?"

He chuckles before responding. "Maybe. But it also might just be the contrast with our ride this morning that's bringing it to the front of your mind. It's hot and there's lots of traffic, and maybe you had your expectations set for something else. You're remembering the "something else," wondering why it's not here today."

I think on that a minute, and realize there's probably a broader truth in what he's saying. We do tend to romanticize the past, and it's easy to be disappointed when the reality of today falls short of the selective version of yesterday we've built in our memories.

"Yeah, but there's more to it than that. There were miserable moments on the ride as well. It's not that I've forgotten those unpleasant memories, but more that in my mind, they just seem like small and incidental details. The overall complexion and feel of the memory is very pleasant. Idealized, really."

Dave chews on the thought for a bit. It's fun to watch Dave think sometimes. He has a wonderful combination of depth and quickness that I often envy. He resists simple answers, to be sure he's dug into the issue far enough, and you can see him wrestling with the conundrum as we make our way up a long and gentle grade. A smile comes across his face as he answers, "It's kind of a neat ability we have, isn't it? I mean, our ability to shape memories like that, so that the *feeling* of the memory is good, even when there were both good and bad in the experience."

Then he turns to me briefly and shrugs, indicating that this might be right or wrong, but it's all he's got. As is common when we're headed up long grades, he tires of my slower pace, and pulls ahead while I keep cogitating.

Since my mind has been so selective in using the bucolic morning joy of the ride as the brush with which to paint the memory, I'm wondering if the joy of the ride was even as good as I'm remembering. How much of my memory of the ride was what really happened, and how much of it did my mind create into the ride it wants to remember, using the best pieces of that ride 35 years ago, and ignoring a few pieces that it didn't like?

Just how much of the life I remember, and that I claim as *me*, is mythology I've created to be the *me* I want to be?

EASTERN KANSAS AND WESTERN MISSOURI

As to scenery (giving my own thought and feeling), while I know the standard claim is that Yosemite, Niagara Falls, the Upper Yellowstone and the like afford the greatest natural shows, I am not so sure but the prairies and plains, while less stunning at first sight, last longer, fill the esthetic sense fuller, precede all the rest, and make North America's characteristic landscape.

Walt Whitman, *Specimen Days,* 1879

COTTONWOOD FALLS, KS

WARRENSBURG, MO

THE FLINT HILLS

*The Flint Hills aren't a place to take your
breath away, they let you catch it.*

Jim Hoy, from *Flint Hills Cowboys*

Most everybody makes jokes about how flat Kansas is. Truthfully, there are some flat stretches of Kansas. Desperately flat stretches that seem to go on forever. Kansas is a big place though, and while the big flat country takes up some of the state, there's surprising diversity in landscape, geology, and habitat.

As for the big flat spaces . . . Well, the Flint Hills are *not* one of those big flat spaces.

The Flint Hills take up a big swath of the state between the big open farm country of central Kansas and the woodlands of the east. The region runs further north to south than it does west to east, extending from the northern border of the state to the southern border. The heart of the region is smack-dab in the middle of the state.

This is the region that William Least Heat-Moon wrote about in his book, *PrairyErth*. It's a part of the country that relatively few people know about, but often those who come and spend any time here fall deeply in love with the place. An ancient mountain range worn down over eons into a vast ocean of deep rolling hills. It's rugged country with rocky soil, and the only areas suitable for farming are the rare bottom-lands where the occasional creek or river winds. For grazing, however, there are few places on earth as rich as the Flint Hills.

I grew up in Kansas and went to college in the heart of the Flint Hills. I have fond memories of bike rides and hikes across these hills from my college days and have hunted in the area many times since. No place on earth feels more like home to me than this region.

I think most of us have a *place* that we call home. Our hearts put roots deeply into the substance of the place, linking us to it forever. Whenever we get close to our home—either in body, mind, or spirit—the *place* sings to us, calling us to reach out and feel the connection.

Riding north along K-177, meandering further and further into the heart of this magical region, I feel the call from my *place*. The song sounds as sweet as that of the grasshopper sparrows that station themselves on fenceposts every hundred yards or so along the road, welcoming me home into the arms of the hills around me.

We ride for many miles along a creek bottom, through the town of Matfield Green, before climbing into the hills again just before we pass Bazaar. Bazaar being a town. Well, not really a town, but a few homes collected together where there once was a town.

In the hills now, with a tailwind, I can't resist the urge to stand on the pedals and crunch up the inclines with everything I have. It feels good to climb hard, out of the saddle, and as I'm about halfway up the first long incline, I notice that the rate at which sweat is raining off me is astounding. There aren't drops of sweat falling *drip drip drip* from my face and head, but rather there's a nearly constant flow. I keep myself lean-ing well over the bars while I'm climbing, to try to keep the stream of sweat from running down my bike. I don't recall having sweat pour off me at quite this rate while riding before. It feels good.

At the top of a little hill, just before descending down toward the town of Cottonwood Falls, we pull into a scenic turnout to enjoy the view and read the history while draining our water bottles. Dave and I never miss one of these scenic turnouts or historical markers. There's history all along the road. Every *place* has its story to tell. These stories should be told.

A little piece of me, though, is chronically outraged at the way history gets told. The winners of the wars write the history books, and that history always gets written in a way that extols the grand virtues of the victors, pities the inferiority of the defeated, and paints a picture of the past that ignores anything that might highlight the atrocities committed to win the war.

This human tendency is evident in the words that most of these roadside markers use, generally telling the story of the European conquest of the continent in one way or another, ignoring the perspective of the people or the land that existed here for eons before our arrival. This marker is no different, and Dave senses my overdeveloped and often misguided sense of justice kicking into overdrive.

"Wasn't it Plato who said something about whoever tells the story rules the world?" he asks playfully.

I think about Dave's comments as I gaze out over the rolling hills beneath the oppressive July heat. "I guess whoever makes the signs gets to make up history. This is something between half-truth and a downright rewriting of history."

Dave thinks it over for a minute, measuring his thoughts, always eager to defuse my irrational zeal with logic. "I don't know," he says. "You don't think any of this is true?"

"They leave out big and important pieces of the truth. The sign makes it appear as though the area was nothing at all until Europeans came and made it this beautiful pastureland. What about the people who lived here on the land before, or the dense diversity of wildlife?"

"I'm not saying your version of the truth isn't valid, Neil. I'm just saying that yours is a version, just like the sign's is a version. It'd be great if we could look out over the hills and see those herds today, but if we could, then we wouldn't be here, would we? We're here because there's this highway, and this highway is here because the area has commercial value as pastureland."

"Yeah I know. I just wish we could tell the whole truth about this stuff rather than always whitewashing what we gave up to get where we are."

"Why? So we can all feel like war criminals? The atrocities our cultural ancestors committed as they stole this land are probably beyond our ability to stomach."

"So we just ignore what they did?"

"I don't know. Were their atrocities any worse than the ones committed by the people who were here before them? *They* took the land from somebody before *them*—I doubt it was a bloodless or gentle process."

"Yeah, I know you're right about that. Maybe it's the scale of what we did that's so troubling. Depending on what version of history you listen to, we committed some form of genocide against the civilizations that lived here before us. And ecologically, who knows how much flora and fauna we decimated into extinction or drove from the land."

"Imagine if there were television documentaries 400 years ago to capture on film what this looked like out here. Probably like those images of the African savannah, covered with all sorts of animals."

"That's exactly what I mean! I don't like that we ignore this stuff—pretend it didn't happen."

"Coping mechanism, I suppose. So let's enjoy the bike ride and keep pedaling without crumbling into a little pile of self-loathing," Dave quips as we climb into the saddles and start slow pedal strokes.

"And somewhere on the other side of the world we're

decimating the African savannah as we speak, refusing to learn from our past mistakes."

"I suppose it's just a matter of scale. Our human nature probably hasn't changed much with the passing of generations, but our technology has. I imagine we've always been a pretty depraved bunch, not afraid of a little genocide or decimation when it suited our immediate needs."

"Yeah, but now we've got technology that can paint long-lasting and unimaginable consequences, and we don't have any idea what to do with it." The tailwind makes it easy to talk as we ride side by side, and Dave nods thoughtfully as we crest the hill and begin to gain some speed coasting. The grade begins to fall away, and as usual my glide is a little faster and I start to pull away.

"We think it's technology we need to harness, but we're wrong. It's our human nature we need to harness as we discover more about bending technology to our will." Dave tosses this last comment to me from behind as I gather speed for a glorious sweep down into the town of Cottonwood Falls.

COTTONWOOD FALLS

Strephon kissed me in the spring,
  Robin in the fall,
But Colin only looked at me
And never kissed at all.

Strephon's kiss was lost in jest,
  Robin's lost in play,
But the kiss in Colin's eyes
Haunts me night and day.

Sara Teasdale, "The Look"

There are a few towns we all run across in our travels that rest in our memories, wrapped in recollections of enchantment. As time passes, our minds steep the memories in spells of mystique. For me, Cottonwood Falls is one of those towns. I recall an old-time main street unspoiled by a modern highway, well-maintained buildings, a thriving small-town community.

The memory of that fanciful place has created my expectation as I coast up to a little convenience store in town. An empty disappointment begins to wash away the sweet memory as I look around and see nothing more than the typical gas station and little store along the highway. Where the heck is the quaint little place I remember?

Our goal for the day has been to make it to either here in Cottonwood Falls or another 20 miles up the road to Council Grove. I remember both as quiet and historic towns—the perfect place for our planned rest day tomorrow. However, looking around for some evidence of the sweet little town I remember from 35 years ago, I resign myself to another 20 miles on the road, hoping that Council Grove doesn't disappoint us.

Our water bottles filled, we continue to coast down the highway to the place where we cross the Cottonwood River. Looking off to my left, I can see that the old downtown is west of the highway, and I wonder if we should have diverted off the road to explore. As we traverse the bridge on the highway, I see a bike path on the left side of the highway, meandering back across an older bridge toward a downtown that the highway no longer penetrates.

Suddenly, my memory snaps back into the right track, and I take a left off the highway, onto the path, and back toward the bridge. I slow and wait for Dave, who rides up with a question on his face.

"What's up?" he asks. "Did you see something?"

"Now I remember. This path is the old highway that crosses the old bridge into town. Are you good with exploring the old town a bit, seeing if there's somewhere we want to stay?"

"Sure. I was wondering if we were missing something. Your description of the town didn't quite match what we were seeing out on the highway."

Memory is like that sometimes. We have such high regard for memory, yet scientists have proven over and over again that our memories are highly pliable and mostly fictional things. We create our memories from the input we receive, and as we create them—in the instant we are creating them—we paint them with our bias, our experience, our worldview, and our current state of mind. Let them steep over the years of our life, and we continually enhance and change them to better match our evolving worldview.

And we do it all subconsciously. We hold tightly to the myth that observation and memory are generally the most valuable evidence of truth. What's more valuable in a trial than an eyewitness? This path into town is a pretty critical piece of the whole picture of Cottonwood Falls, yet my memory had erased it completely, retrieving it only when slapped in the face with the image. And even then, do I really remember it, or did my disappointment make me so desperate that I'm willing to convince myself that I'm now remembering it?

Typing these words, at an age and a point in life where memories fail me more often than I like to admit, I'm comforted by the understanding that even in our prime, the strength, value, and voracity of our memories are mostly myths.

It's a beautiful old bridge that leads us back across the quiet Cottonwood River and into the wonderful old town of Cottonwood Falls that I remember. The first thing we come to in the old town is the Millstream Resort Motel, right on the banks of the river. We pull in and chat a bit with Sharon, the proprietor, and settle on a room for two nights, looking forward to a rest day in small-town America.

After a hot shower and a stroll around town, Dave and I enjoy a giant hunk of steak at the historic old Grand Central Hotel and Grill. Chatting as we eat, I feel the value of Dave's friendship. True and good friends are a treasure, a treasure that I didn't really understand well enough earlier in life. Sitting in this grand old hotel, relaxing after a hot day in the saddle, deeper understanding seeps into me. Sharing a beer, filling ourselves with steak, chatting about the adventure we're sharing, the treasure of my friendship with Dave clarifies in my mind. I see it as something more lucid and tangible. Like the "Magic Eye" images, where the picture hidden within the picture suddenly jumps out at you, and you wonder how it wasn't clear before.

HUNTING WITH BEETHOVEN

When we pay attention to nature's music, we find that everything on the Earth contributes to its harmony.

Hazrat Inayat Khan

The air is still and heavy early the next morning as I sit out on the back deck at the Millstream. The sky is dark at this predawn hour, the soft sound of the river adding an easygoing background to this cherished hour of the day. Moonlight filters down through the trees hanging over the river, and I notice a man is sitting on a lawn chair on the old bridge that crosses the river. Filtered shafts from the light of the moon dance along the length of a fishing pole that hangs out over the bridge in front of him.

Catfishing. A midwestern oddity I grew up with, and still find curious.

Mind you, I love to fish. But fishing takes on many flavors, and this is one of the flavors for which I've never developed a taste. I generally enjoy a more active style of fishing. I might spend hours in my boat, quietly trolling along a shore, searching out that perfect combination of conditions, hunting, pursuing.

I'll cast my line hundreds of times up against the bank, or into promising habitat. I might catch some fish, or I might not get a single bite. But I'm fishing and enjoying myself.

Something about fishing infects some of us, and pulls us back to it over and over. It doesn't seem to be (as logic might suggest) connected all that much to the actual catching of fish (though catching fish certainly enhances the experience). It's some special combination of factors that stack up to a complete gestalt of fishing. It's this gestalt that defines the fishing experience for us. I can describe some of the pieces that make up the whole, but the actual thing that keeps us coming back is much more than just a sum of factors.

There's the peace, tranquility, and thoughtful space that usually surrounds the act of fishing. While not always part of the sport, it's a pretty common component. Some of this peace and tranquility comes from the world around you, but some of it comes from within as a response to where you are, both mentally and physically. It's an opportunity to clear your mind of extraneous noise, and give yourself completely to the space you're in and your place within that space.

For me, fishing is mostly about this peace and tranquility of the space within *and* the space without, combined with "the hunt." Fishing feels more like art than sport to me. It becomes a *place* I go to, a place I paint in my heart and soul with that palette of the conservative heart and the longings of the hunter's soul, with a brush built from the beauty of the space I occupy when I fish.

But when it comes to catfishing, the canvas stays blank.

In college I had a neighbor who went down to the creek (or "crick," depending on your dialect) to fish for catfish every summer evening as the sun went down. He'd spend most of the night down there, come back to sleep a few hours, and head off to work in the morning. I'm an early riser, and remember many mornings when I'd be studying at 4:00 a.m. and I'd see the shadow of his return through my backyard. I suspect he must have slept on the bank of the creek at least part of that time, but I never knew for sure.

He eventually confided that the real attraction to fishing for him was that it allowed him to get out of the house and spend some time alone. I guess it was his escape—maybe a way of avoiding conflict. I'm thinking there must be more effective ways of solving that particular problem, but then again, I suppose marriage counseling can get expensive, and I'm certainly not one to dispense any advice in that area.

The first hints of dawn in the eastern sky drop tiny shreds of light through the canopy of trees above and down onto the bridge The figure of the catfishing occupant becomes more clear, softened by the light mist that rolls up from the river below and over the bridge. Dave joins me on the back porch, and we drift into the comfortable conversation of good friends, accompanied by the growing symphony of birds from the trees that surround the river and the Millstream.

"Good morning," Dave greets me as he settles into a chair beside me.

"Morning."

"I thought you were still sleeping—I've been in there reading for a bit."

"Yeah, was awake early, just enjoying a gorgeous start to the day."

We sit quietly in the moist morning air. Dave notices the fella sitting on the bridge and asks, "Is that somebody sitting on the bridge?"

"Yeah, I imagine he's fishing for catfish."

"Do you think he's catching any?"

"Probably not. Guys sit there with lines in the water for hours sometimes." I pause a minute, then relate the story of my neighbor in college.

Dave has this slightly crooked smile he gets when he's trying to piece together something he doesn't quite understand. His head cocks a bit as he starts to respond, but he ends up shaking his head in a gesture that means something like, "I don't know what to say." He continues to watch the motionless man in the lawn chair sitting on the bridge, then asks, "You like to fish, don't you?"

"I do, but not really catfishing. A little too sedentary. The kind of fishing I like is more like hunting; pursuing the fish, trying to find it and figure it out." After a pause, I add, "Do you fish at all?"

"Nope. Nothing about it interests me."

Dave doesn't hunt either. I, on the other hand, can get pretty passionate about hunting. There are things that are part of the hunting experience that pull at me with such force that I can never imagine how a person couldn't find the excitement in them. Learning to be quiet and unobtrusive, to blend and become part of the habitat. Discovering how to use all my senses more fully—sight, sound, scent, and the unconscious brain telling me things my conscious brain can't understand. Learning the habits and behavior of the prey, becoming good at finding and stalking. The silence of the bow, the satisfaction of a well placed shot. Not to mention the bonus of excellent and healthy food for the table.

Dave just shakes his head at that stuff. Once, while Dave and I were hiking in the mountains above Leadville, Colorado, I smelled elk close to us. I let Dave know, and we were able to stalk up to within 10 or 20 yards of a nice bull elk who was resting in a little ravine. Then, as we continued our hike, I pointed out a place where deer had recently bedded down, based on the sign and the fresh smell.

To me, this was thrilling. I was absolutely positive that the hunting bug would infect Dave after this, and he'd want to start hunting. These were things that were so exciting to me that I couldn't begin to fathom that someone else wouldn't become hooked on the full hunting experience.

I suppose that if Beethoven were alive, and he sat me down and played the piano for me, I'd appreciate that it sounded really nice, but it probably wouldn't change my life. I'd be likely to learn a little more about the music, and learn new ways to appreciate it, but I wouldn't spend my life learning to compose music or play the piano as a result of the encounter. I'd say something like, "Very nice, Ludwig, thanks for sharing. That was amazing. Hey, can I get you a beer?"

Music lovers are cringing right now, I know. How could I possibly not see and feel and hear the indescribable beauty and passion in the music performed by that master?

I think that after our hike in the mountains that day Dave appreciated that the experience was fun, appreciated that in other circumstances he would have walked right past the elk, or right past the place where it had been before his approach scared it off. He appreciated that we were able to smell it ahead of time and quietly make our way right up to it—to experience wildlife in a way he hadn't really before. When we got back to our cabin, I'm sure he expressed some appreciation. He probably said something like, "Very nice, Neil, thanks for sharing. That was amazing. Hey, can I get you a beer?"

And I probably said sure, enjoyed the beer with him, and to this day remain flummoxed that there are people on earth who aren't ardently thrilled by the gestalt of a good hunting experience, becoming one with the environment around you, finding the harmony and balance of our *place* in the wilderness.

TENNIS ON THE BACK PORCH

*The great virtue of my radicalism lies in the fact
that I am perfectly ready, if necessary, to be radical
on the conservative side.*

Teddy Roosevelt

Dave and I sit quietly for many minutes, enjoying the sounds
of the river below dancing up at us. An early morning sky begins the slow bloom of light, showing itself above us in tiny
pieces through the cottonwood leaves.

"So here's a question for you." Dave has a smile on his
face that says he's serving something up. It's a smile that reminds me of a smile a girlfriend in college would give me just
before she rocketed a serve across the net on the tennis court.
She was quite good at tennis—on the college tennis team, I
believe—and I was just trying to learn. Well actually, I didn't
really care so much about learning tennis as I did about using
it as an excuse to spend time around her.

Dave continues with his question while I recall that smile
from the tennis court many years ago. "How is it that hunters

and fishermen talk about being conservationists, when what they're really doing is taking stuff out of the habitat? How is *taking* the same as *conserving*?"

That college girlfriend had a certain smug twitch at the corner of her mouth whenever I wasn't able to handle her serve. Okay, out of respect for accuracy, using the term *girlfriend* to refer to her probably stretches the truth. She was a friend, who was a girl. I was a boy in my early 20s, obsessed enough with her to get spanked on the tennis court each week just for the chance to be close to her.

Dave never gets a twitch like that at the corner of his mouth. Discussion with us is never a contest. There's certainly a bit of volleying back and forth during our discussions, the occasional rocket launched across the net, but there's enough trust and respect that discussions are mostly about learning from each other. If we agree on something there's usually not much discussion, but if we disagree, we both see it as a chance to learn a new perspective.

I think for a few minutes, chewing on the question with one side of my brain, while the other side is wondering what ever happened to that girl who used to kick my ass on the tennis court. "Well, I think hunting can be an important part of conservation, when regulated wisely and executed with care. I'm not sure about fishing . . . Maybe fishing too." I pause while I continue to think. Dave knows I'm still thinking, and rather than jumping in, he waits with me until my little brain has put together the next sentence. "But the thing is, I think it's too broad a brush to say that all hunting or all fishing is conservation. I don't think *all* hunting and fishing is conservation, but *some of it* can be."

"But how can any of it be, really? Are you really conserving anything? You're going out and taking something, right?"

"Two ways, I think. The first way is money. Every time I buy a hunting or fishing license I'm essentially paying a tax to help the state's conservation efforts. The conservation efforts are often aimed at building and maintaining wildlife habitat.

The whole truth is that a good deal of that habitat and effort is built and maintained largely so guys like me can hunt on it, but is that a wholly bad thing? It gets built and maintained, right?"

"Good point. I agree; that's a good thing. How much money are we talking about? What's a hunting license cost?"

"Depends on the state, and depends on whether you're a resident or nonresident. As a resident in Colorado, I probably spend between $100 and $200 a year on my licenses and tags to hunt in Colorado. But I hunt quite a bit. Plus, in Kansas, I give them more than $400 a year to hunt and fish as a nonresident."

"That's a ton! I had no idea people spent so much money to hunt and fish."

"And in a lot of ways, it's the perfect tax. I'm being taxed, but specifically for the activities I like to do, right? There are lots of things I don't mind supporting and am happy to support with taxes, but some things are pretty hard to support, and we really have no choice on where our money is spent with broad taxes like income taxes and sales taxes."

"And you think all that money the states collect for licenses is spent wisely?"

"Probably not. Probably like any bureaucracy—private or public—a ton of it gets wasted. But at the end of the day, there's more good wildlife habitat for us all to enjoy. Some of us enjoy it during hunting and fishing season, but there are probably a whole lot of folks who don't even like the idea of hunting or fishing who end up enjoying the benefits that are paid for by hunters and fishermen."

The porch is quiet for a few minutes while we enjoy the sunlight that's now dappling the tops of the trees, stirring a tiny breeze through the cottonwood leaves. As a hunter and fisherman, I can't let the discussion end without one final admission.

"Truth is that some portion of hunters and fishermen are slobs. They hunt in sloppy ways, waste game, destroy habitat. They have no regard for the concept of *fair chase* or *conservation,* and I'm ashamed when I see their behavior. I like to think it's a small percentage of the total, but I really have no way of knowing. They're the ones who give us all a bad name. There's nothing conservative about them, and it's a travesty when they call themselves conservationists."

"I suppose there are the exceptions in any group—folks who give the rest a bad name. It's a shame the exceptions are always the ones the media focuses on, giving the general public a slanted and unrealistic view." Dave pauses for a minute, then continues. "So you said you thought there were two ways that hunters are conservationists. What's the second way?"

"Oh yeah. Well it's the obvious, really. Assuming a well managed wildlife resource, and accepting that natural predation on many species no longer exists, the hunter is the predator that keeps wildlife populations at a healthy level. Shut down hunting and some species will overpopulate to levels that are unhealthy to the animal as well as dangerous to us and to them."

"Yeah, I see that one. Back at Dad's farm there are some years when it's dangerous to take the car out at night. My mom won't even drive at night anymore for fear of hitting a deer."

The fella fishing on the bridge hasn't moved a bit, and I'm pretty sure he's sleeping. Low shafts of sunlight push through the mist that rolls across the bridge from the river below. The still morning air is warm and humid, promising another sweltering Kansas July day.

Dave's feet are propped up on the porch rail, and I slouch down in my chair and kick my feet up too, before asking, "I wonder if the little café in town is open for breakfast yet?"

"You'd think so. Must be close to 6:00." Then after a pause, he continues, "On the other hand, it seems like a quirky little town—they might not open until 7:00. You want to wander down there and see?"

"I'm good waiting 'til 7:00. I'm really enjoying this back porch."

Dave smiles and agrees. He's still got that thoughtful look on his face like he's chewing on our earlier conversation.

The tennis ball is still going back and forth over the net, and he's not ready for this set to end. He puts a little spin on his next serve: "So, as with all things, big money must influence decisions on conservation, right? In this case, where does the money come from? Who's influencing the policy-making?"

His question launches us into discussion that meanders through terrain we've explored many times, analyzing the many ways that Big Money corrupts the democratic process and undermines the potential virtue and decency that government is capable of.

As is generally the case, I'm probably overly cynical regarding the ability of a corporation to behave in a socially responsible manner unless such behavior will promote the reason for the existence of the corporation in the first place: to generate wealth for the shareholders. At the same time, Dave is probably overly optimistic about the likelihood that the basic goodness of the human spirit will outshine personal greed and that private enterprise can be guided by some sort of moral compass.

There are good arguments to be made on both sides of the discussion, and our verbal walkabout occasionally wanders across the line into emotionally charged territory. As usual, we don't resolve differences in opinion, but we understand and respect both sides, meandering to a place that feels like a good place of closure.

"I don't buy it Neil. I think people will make the right decision at the end of the day, even if it's contrary to the profit motive. Maybe not all people, but most people."

"You might be right. I'm just saying that structurally, we've set things up to make it difficult to make those right decisions. As a corporate officer, I'm bound by law to help my shareholders make profit, and my personal financial incentives are almost always lined up very closely with that objective. My conscience might have a hard time being heard in the face of those demands and incentives."

"I know it's naive, but I want to believe in the overarching goodness of the human spirit."

"I do too . . . "

We sit quietly for a while, letting the feelings of conflict subside as we ease back into the comfort of our friendship. The tennis ball has come to rest by the net, and we seem to have agreed that the match is over. Neither of us has any idea what the score is; we weren't keeping track.

My girlfriend (remember I use that term loosely) in college kept track of the score. There was never any doubt in my mind that she was keeping track. But, whether out of respect for my fragile male ego or out of pure graciousness—possibly both—she never actually voiced the score when we were done playing. We'd meet at the net in the middle of the court, and she'd pretend not to know what the score was.

But I knew she knew, and she knew that I knew that she knew.

Then, in keeping with her infinite graciousness, she'd accept my invitation to walk down to the Baskin-Robbins on the edge of Aggieville, and I'd buy her an ice cream. Back in those olden days, we called that a date. Well, at least I called it a date. A painfully shy introvert, I never did figure out how to ask that girl out on a real date. We just had ice cream together.

Except for one beautiful summer day, and a wonderful ride on my motorcycle. We meandered through the folds of the Flint Hills on two wheels, finding a shady place beside a stream to spend time being alone and close, getting to know one another. We found the edge of a precipice that day, a precipice we both knew we could tumble across into something neither of us was ready for.

Just one summer afternoon.

It was 35 years before I asked her out on a real date. She suggested some tennis, but we settled on some hiking and biking.

But it's not time for that story yet . . .

Sunlight bathes the bridge now, burning off the last of the fog rolling along the river below. Our catfisherman is gathering up his gear, clearly done for the morning. There's a little café in town that's calling our name, and we gather up our stuff and head toward it.

EMMA CHASE

But I, when I undress me
Each night, upon my knees
Will ask the Lord to bless me
With apple-pie and cheese.

Eugene Field

I'm pleased to report that the pie at the Emma Chase Cafe is, indeed, good pie. I've had some mighty fine pie in my life—pie so good it's called Pretty Good Pie—so the bar is pretty high when you ask me to evaluate pie. The Emma Chase pie can't compare to Pretty Good Pie, but it's pretty good nonetheless.

Not that anyone has asked me this morning to evaluate pie, but since they seemed to think so much of their pie, I felt duty bound to at least try it. Not to worry though, I had a healthy breakfast of chicken-fried steak and eggs before indulging in the pie.

Dave had a quick breakfast with me, then left before the pie to explore the little town on his own while I relax at the diner. I know I'll be getting out and exploring, but there's a warm and homey feel to the Emma Chase diner this morning that I don't want to let go of.

The fictional town of Cicely was home to a TV series called *Northern Exposure*. It was a quirky show where an extremely diverse group of people came together to create a fun and harmonious culture. The peace just seemed to work. I'm remembering that series as I listen to the conversations around me at the Emma Chase this morning.

A political discussion between four old fellas rages at a table not far away. It's clear that three of the guys are big fans of the right wing, and one fella is a fan of the left wing. The three right-wing fellas are hitting the left winger with every soundbite in the book, and the left winger just keeps coming back with questions. I'm impressed with a couple of different things as I listen to the conversation.

First is the thought that I might be observing a basic difference between the right-wing mindset and the left-wing mindset here at the table. Could it be that folks who lean right tend to like answers, and folks who lean left tend to like questions? In many ways this makes sense to me. Folks who don't like ambiguity do seem to lean to the right, craving simple answers and clear direction. Folks who eschew overt authority and have endless questions seem to lean left.

I'll observe here that the above oversimplification appeals to the left half of my brain, which wants to lean right. At the same time, the fact that I pose it as a question clearly appeals to the right half of my brain, which leans endlessly left . . .

The second (and more important) thing that impresses me as I listen is the nature of the relationship these fellas have. They're clearly all friends and seem to respect each other. They're throwing hardballs and not giving any quarter. It's refreshing to see and hear this ability to have respectful discourse. There's no name calling, and no assuming that someone must be stupid if they have a different opinion.

These are four guys who know each other well and have probably known each other for many years—maybe all their lives. They can't insult each other and walk away; they'll all be back at the same table tomorrow sharing breakfast again.

They're *community*, and like it or not, they have to get along at some level.

Community politics is unique in a small town. In the wider world, it's too easy to call somebody a moron and walk away. It's painfully easy for some talking head on TV to yell over the top of somebody and make them out to be idiotic for having a different opinion. Communication happens via email, or Facebook, or Twitter, or whatever the newest method is to keep distance between real people.

Here at the Emma Chase, there are no smart phones. There are just real people, sitting together at the breakfast table, having real discussions. They're face to face, eyeball to eyeball. The person sitting across from them is their friend, and the person is more important than the ideology. Somebody will buy somebody coffee this morning, and it's possible somebody will think about what was said earlier at the breakfast table, and they might expand their perspective just a little bit.

I think of Dave again, and I'm thankful once again for the friendship we have. The rarity of friends with whom we can have real "converse-ation" strikes me, and I realize how lucky I am to have such a friend. I wonder if these guys at the table realize how lucky they are.

Eventually I run out of excuses to sit in the café. The old women in the middle of the room are knitting in earnest, having their own conversation, and the old men at the table eventually wander off to their day. I pay my tab and make my way out into the Kansas heat, eager for a day of exploration in this beautiful old town. By the time the afternoon heat drives Dave and me off the streets, the shade on the back porch at the Millstream will be calling our names. We'll enjoy our pa-laver, bantering back and forth across the net, learning new and different ways to look at something we might already have an opinion on.

And really, there's not much I don't already have an opin-ion on . . .

MOURNING SONG

As I looked about me I felt that the grass was the country, as the water is the sea. The red of the grass made all the great prairie the colour of winestains, or of certain seaweeds when they are first washed up. And there was so much motion in it; the whole country seemed, somehow, to be running.

Willa Cather, *My Ántonia*

DAY 22 • COTTONWOOD FALLS TO OTTAWA, KANSAS

Thunderstorms rolled through the Flint Hills overnight, leaving the air damp and heavy. We strap our bags onto our bikes in the predawn darkness, breathing in the light fog around us. I sense a heavy fog hanging above, between me and the sky. Some combination of sight and sound and smell makes that layer apparent in the dark. I've often wondered how we know it's there, but we're good at sensing it.

There's a hauntingly quiet quality to the sound of riding your bike down the streets of a small town early in the morning. Nobody's up yet, there's no light, and the sound of the tires on the road and the chain as it turns bounces a lonely feel off the walls of the homes as I pass. This morning the feeling is enhanced by the fog that shrouds me as I ride.

As usual, Dave is a hundred yards or so in front of me, starting to crank the pace up. The warmth feels good in my legs as they start to work harder. My lungs relish the moist morning air as I draw it deeply into myself. My heart pounds in my chest with a rhythm that is slowly accelerating.

I don't have a good singing voice, but I'm passable at harmonizing with other voices. When I've sung with folks in the past, especially when singing a capella, there's a sweetness that happens when the voices come into tune with one another. It usually doesn't happen with the first note, but rather it's a progression that starts with folks struggling to find the right pitch. You steal sideways glances at other singers, and might see a furrowed brow now and again. Folks are leaning away from the other voices to avoid distraction. Then, as the music progresses, you hit a spot here and there where the voices come together nicely. From these little spots of good harmony coming together, smiles start to creep onto faces, wrinkles smooth out of brows, and tension is replaced by relaxation. You start to sing *with your ears,* your vocal cords and ears connecting unconsciously. Most of the time, this is as far as it gets—a few really wonderful spots where the harmony is just right, surrounded by music that's close enough to right to sound pleasant.

But now and again, something happens that feels like a little piece of heaven. The voices come together in a delicious harmony, and they stay there. When this happens, eyes close, and everyone leans together so they can better hear the voice as a whole. Instead of four voices, the sound becomes a single voice. If you're lucky enough to be part of that when it happens, it makes the hair on the back of your neck stand up. You feel chills all the way to your toes. You never want the singing to stop. When it does stop, you feel a powerful connection to the others in the group.

There's a sweet spot a little like this that can happen on a bicycle. It happens when the ride is pleasant, you feel good, the surroundings are nice, the weather is just right—essentially everything around you and about the ride is good. Then the riding itself starts to find the tune. You slowly crank the effort up to find that spot where lungs and heart and muscles all work hard together, balancing with a pedal cadence that feels right. Everything falls into place perfectly, harmony wraps itself around you, and you never want the ride to end.

Riding along this beautiful stretch of rolling highway, the hills around me emerging from the early morning twilight fog, the sound of prairie birds floating across the heavy air, I find myself searching for that harmony, finding it briefly now and then, falling into the little slice of heaven that's happening around me.

Pedal, breathe, smile, and enjoy.

On both sides of me as I ride is the Tallgrass Prairie National Preserve. The preserve was a dream of conservationists back when I was going to college in the area. In the end, well-intentioned people on both sides of sometimes-hot debates came together to find a little harmony; to compromise. They were all conservative in the truest sense—Teddy Roosevelt conservatives—who wanted to be sure that we didn't lose a treasure. They all agreed that we needed to behave as responsible stewards, and found a way to navigate through political differences to solve a problem.

The harmony of good intentions won out over the dissonance of ego, and the preserve came to be.

Real progress. Progressive. Conservative. Together. Tell me again the difference?

Knowing this history, the tallgrass prairie on both sides of me feels even more significant. While the vast prairie that was a blanket across the Great Plains has faded into history, this remnant of that treasure survives here in these hills that feel so special to me. I'm finding myself feeling deep nostalgia about this as I glide along the rolling highway, working hard, clipping along nicely, surrounded by a harmony emerging from that sublime balance of exertion and progress.

And regret. I'm feeling regret, and wondering where it's coming from.

Funny how those feelings so often come together. Sweet harmony playing off the dissonance of nostalgia and regret. The dissonance of emotions settles through me, and I realize that there's more to what's happening as I roll along this lonely highway than simple regret that so much of the prairie was devoured by change.

A bittersweet sadness from a deeply personal place boils up inside me. It's a powerful melancholy that spills over into my thoughts and emotions as I ride, rising out of an emotional tank that I generally keep tightly contained.

My marriage of 30 years is slowly dissolving, and my wife and I don't seem to be able to find a way to stop it. There isn't any hatred, or an event to define an unavoidable end, but rather a slow but inexorable march away from each other. Seeing the prairie around me in this misty light, understanding that this little slice of prairie is all that's left of what was once a vast treasure, reminds me of a treasure in my life that's being devoured by the grind of time.

I know this isn't an uncommon pattern to a marriage. A couple comes together, raises a family, and fails to find a way to assure that their relationship evolves in a sustainable way through it all. We spend ourselves on the important tasks of raising children, making a living, and giving ourselves to the community. We allow ourselves to be consumed by the day-to-day demands and necessities of life. Then one day, after the kids are gone and things are settling down, you look across the table at each other and realize that the lives you've each built are only together because it's a convenient habit.

Nothing at all like marriages that come apart because of some infraction on the part of one party or the other. There's no treacherous deed, no incendiary action, no unforgivable word. Things like that might actually be more understandable, or more fixable. Instead, it's a slow unwinding that a couple allows to occur. Inaction more than action. Silence more than words.

I suppose if a marriage came apart because of some thing that happened, then one or both people would feel anger. Maybe there would be hate or vitriol or fury or indignation. All emotions that would be understandable as part of a breakup.

But I don't feel any of that, and I don't believe she does either. What I feel is a giant hole. A void where something once existed, but no longer does. A deep and quiet grief for things not said, emotions not expressed, feelings not declared.

Profound sadness.

Heartrending regret.

While some marriages survive this, and the partners find a way to reshape and redefine themselves and their relationship in a way that fits together in the new world that they're part of, there are many marriages that can't find their way over this hurdle. I suspect it's not easy to do, since we're all changed by the life we move through. With each passing month, my marriage feels less and less like one that will clear the hurdle.

Melancholy. Is that what I'm feeling? Is it because I'm riding through this little slice of the world I call home? Because this all feels safe to me? Maybe the morning fog drifting across the hills evokes a sense of looking back into the past and feeling past missteps, slights, and failures peeking at me through the mist.

A tiny little riff of mourning. An unexpected dissonant interval in this beautiful morning song.

But like so often in music, the dissonance stands out as a contrast to the consonance in the song. Alongside the crushing regret for things not said or done are marvelous successes and wonderful memories. The melancholy I feel isn't gloomy or grim. It's bittersweet.

Life needs to move on. But this morning I find myself back at the place I call home, sailing through beautiful rolling hills shrouded in misty dawn light, emboldened by hard work, enjoying air that's moist and cool, hearing a song of morning beauty. The moisture on my cheeks doesn't come from that foggy morning air, but from mournful notes of regret I feel deep in my soul.

By the time Dave and I glide down the long slope into Council Grove, the mist has burned off of the morning, and my cheeks have dried. We find a great little diner on the east side of town called the Saddlerock Cafe, where we sit down to a heaping plate of chicken-fried steak, eggs, and potatoes. We're close to the Big Table, and we enjoy observing small-town culture as the local fellas rotate through and enjoy their coffee.

Things change. Does timelessness exist only in the enduring rhythm of change? One fella finishes his coffee and leaves, another sits down in his chair, reaching for a mug to fill.

TRANSITION

Everything changes but change itself. Everything flows
and nothing remains the same . . . You cannot step twice
into the same river, for other waters and yet others go
flowing ever on.

Heraclitus

Council Grove is a hub in this story, from which two spokes emerge. On the first of those spokes, Dave and I rode down into town on that nostalgic July morning in 2010 and had breakfast at the Saddlerock Cafe, then continued our journey in Kansas for a few more days. After breakfast, we saddled up and continued north on K-177 toward Manhattan, Kansas. Up the road a ways, we turned left and headed back west on K-4, enjoying a transition out of the grasslands of the Flint Hills and into lush central Kansas farm country. We ended our journey in central Kansas after a couple more days of pleasant riding.

Two years later a different spoke emerges. It's September of 2012, and I'm back in Council Grove. In the two years that have elapsed, my wife and I did indeed end our marriage, though we're still close friends. She's dropping me off in Council Grove on her way to visit friends in southern Missouri. On the drive, and over dinner, we have conversations that aren't easy. Conversations that reflect the heartbreak in the ending of a 30-year marriage. We find a way to see each other through the pain, and hold each other, and say good-bye.

It's funny how spokes interconnect as we move through time, weaving the wheel that is the life we live. I'm learning to define my relationship with the woman I was married to for 30 years as one of friendship rather than matrimony. I'm coming to learn that there's building that needs to happen in a divorce just like there is in a marriage. As the marriage comes apart, the relationship needs to build as each person comes to mean something different to the person who was once a spouse. It's neither simple nor easy.

In the predawn darkness of a September morning, I climb into the saddle in Council Grove, alone, and begin pedaling east through a very light autumn mist. I'm beginning the final leg of my journey across the country, focused on the road in front of me, my legs beginning to warm with a little exertion.

The mirror on my helmet is fogged by a light morning mist, shrouding the view behind me. Sometimes the road behind is less clear than the road ahead, fogged by the swirl of emotion. Layers of joyful memories and painful regrets obscure the path, but I fail to see the symbolism of this moment of departing.

The lights are on at the Saddlerock Cafe as I pedal past. I turn the cranks hard in the early morning chill, building my heartbeat, searching for that sweet spot of harmony.

Pedaling out onto the open road, alone.

Pedal, breathe, smile, and enjoy.

JEFF IN OSAGE CITY

One travels more usefully when alone,
because he reflects more.

Thomas Jefferson

The occasional car passes as I make my way east along US 56, giving me plenty of space as they do, in keeping with my experiences so far on the highways in Kansas. The highway here is an evolution of what was once the Santa Fe Trail, a big enough highway that I was concerned that traffic might be heavier. For a good portion of the 70 miles I'll ride today, there's a bike trail that parallels the highway. However, when I checked out the trailhead yesterday, it looked like it was crushed rock rather than paved path, so I've elected to stay on the shoulder of the highway.

Each time I catch a glimpse of the bike path when it gets close to the road, I wonder if I should move over there and try it out. The morning sun is right in front of me, and I worry about cars coming up behind me with the sunlight in their eyes. The bike path would be safer, but there's that unknown thing of the surface, how smooth it would be, whether the gravel would slow me down . . . I come to one point where it would be really easy to move over to the bike trail, but at that exact moment, conditions on my highway are really good, and I ride right past.

Plus there's the whole speed thing. I'm making really good time, even though there is a crosswind. I'll be meeting my brother in Ottawa this evening, and I'll feel particularly good if I make great time on this first day. There's a whole bunch of "giddy-up-and-go" in my tank, and there's too much I don't know about the bike path.

We're like that. The road we're on is always the easy road to ride. It might actually be less healthy for us than we realize, or there may be a different road not far away that we really need to be on, but we're creatures of habit and pattern, and we'll almost always stay on the current path when faced with a choice. Sometimes in the face of overwhelming evidence that we need to get on a different path, we'll go to great lengths to justify our current path.

The gravel might get a little rough and slow us down.

By the time I get to Osage City, my water bottles are bone dry. It's turning into a hot September day, and I spend a good deal of time relaxing under the awning at the convenience store while I take in plenty of water. While I'm relaxing in the shade, a young fella walks up to me and starts a conversation.

"Where ya ridin' to?"

"Headed to Ottawa today." As I watch him, he seems interested in hearing more, so I keep going. "I'm actually headed across the country, and just this morning I started the last leg of the journey in Council Grove, with the plan to end in Annapolis in two weeks."

"Wow! Two weeks? So how long does the whole trip from coast to coast take—four weeks?"

"I haven't really counted up the days, but I'm a little over halfway now, so maybe closer to five weeks?"

He circles my bike, looking it up and down. "My name's Jeff," he says as he sticks out his hand to shake.

"Mine's Neil. Glad to meet you, Jeff."

"You're travelin' pretty light—does someone follow you with more gear?"

"Nope, just me. I've got it trimmed down to the bare essentials, don't I?"

"Man, I'll say." He pauses while continuing to look the bike over. "Ya know, I used to ride quite a bit. All over this area really. I'd do hundred-mile days all the time. Then I got run off the road, so I don't ride much anymore."

"Run off the road? You mean by a car?"

"Yeah, some guy ran me right off the road. Came by and clipped me with the mirror on his pickup. Nobody else on the road, and he knocks me off the road. You gotta watch out for some of these yahoos!"

"Really? He hit you? Did you get hurt?"

"Oh yeah. Broke my collarbone, and messed up my back. Haven't been on a bike since."

Anybody who's ridden on the road for a while has stories like this. Drivers who maliciously run cyclists off the road or throw things at them. To add insult to injury, there are rarely any consequences for the perpetrators; almost never is there any level of prosecution. I'm thinking about this as I probe more.

"So what happened? You went to the hospital? Did the driver get charged with anything?"

"Yeah, the ambulance came and took me to the hospital. But I didn't have any health insurance at the time, so I didn't want them to spend much time looking me over—I couldn't afford any big doctor bills."

"Wouldn't his insurance company pay for it? I mean, he ran you off the road. I would think his insurance company would want to settle this with you. He did get charged with something, right?"

"Nah. They said it was really his word against mine, and

his story was that I was taking up too much of the lane and swerved out into his truck. So the cops never even wrote him a ticket. I guess I could have tried to fight it, but I couldn't afford the hospital bill, let alone a lawyer."

I shake my head as I think about this. If the driver of a vehicle hits a pedestrian, a highway worker, another car, almost anything other than a cyclist, there are tickets written or charges filed. The vehicle driver is usually assumed to have done something wrong, in allowing their vehicle to injure someone else. Yet when a cyclist is involved in the accident, the story is too often similar to Jeff's story. No charges filed, another cyclist injured, no cultural or legal pressure for drivers to have any concern for the safety of cyclists on the road.

This is really becoming an epidemic in America. Hate radio has all sorts of talking heads who will incite anger toward cyclists in general, so there's some (not insignificant) portion of American drivers who feel justified in behaving poorly or downright criminally toward cyclists on the road. With the explosion of texting while driving, the problem is just getting worse.

It's a sad commentary on the state of civility in our nation when such a level of cowardly and abusive behavior is so common. I have no doubt it's a small percentage of people who behave like this, but the fact that there is rarely any criminal or civil action taken against them when they are caught only encourages the conduct. Like any other criminal act, it only stops when the culture won't tolerate it any more, which means severe consequences have to accompany the actions.

What causes the behavior in the first place? Are there folks who hate anyone on a bicycle? Or maybe jealous of anyone who's trying to keep themselves in good shape? I'm sure some folks are just such craven cowards that they get off on attacking someone much smaller and more vulnerable than they are, someone who can't possibly retaliate. Tiny little people who use bullying to make themselves feel bigger.

Jeff is still looking over my bike and my gear, asking a question now and then about the sorts of things I pack. He eventually steps into the store to pay for his gas, and we bid our farewells as he walks back past me toward his car. Watching him walk away, I notice the limp and care in his step, and wonder if the driver who ran him off the road ever regrets what he did to this man.

BUBBA

*When brothers agree, no fortress is
so strong as their common life.*

Antisthenes

The hot, sticky Kansas air has soaked deep into me as I pedal
into Ottawa, feeling strong after 70 miles of pedaling hard.
My brother Erik has driven down from Kansas City to share
supper with me, and we end up opting for the easy choice
and trying one of those cheap "steakhouse" chains. Our first
chunks of meat are too tough to chew or swallow, so we ask
for replacements while we wade through the side dishes.

Born and raised in Kansas, Erik and I were both suckled
in the "heart of niceness," as Garrison Keillor might say. We're
polite to the young kid whom we send back to the kitchen
with the overcooked leather on plates, assuring him that he's
doing a great job, but that we really need the kitchen to do a
better job next time. He's equally polite in apologizing as he
ambles away with the small shuffling steps high school boys
are required to take these days to keep their pants from falling down off their hips. I'm certain somebody, someday, will

invent a device to help these poor young fellows, something that will hold their pants up on top of their hips, and let them move normally through life. Something that will belt their pants more tightly to their waists.

"You think this is their strategy to save on the cost of meat?" Erik asks as he shakes his head watching the poor young fellow struggle toward the kitchen, stopping occasionally to reach down and hitch one side of his pants up a bit, since they're just barely staying up.

"You mean to send out a first cut so tough you have to send it back, then you fill up on potatoes waiting for the next piece to get here?" I respond.

"Right."

"Which would be okay if the sides were decent. But really, these peas must have been boiled into oblivion sometime last year, then kept warm here waiting for me and my plate."

"Yeah," Erik responds with a chuckling grunt. "I just don't get it. How do these places stay in business? Look around at the people in here—they can't possibly think this is decent fare, or worth the price."

"I wonder about that often. I mean, we'll spend maybe $25 or so each here, including a couple of beers and a tip. A decent place that served decent meat in a small town like this might charge $30 or $40 each for a good steak and good beer. A difference of $5 to $15 is nothing."

"Half the people in here probably spent that on cigarettes or lottery tickets this afternoon."

"Right. But somehow they have it in their minds that saving those few bucks is worth putting up with a meal that's mediocre at best."

"Not to start with the psychobabble, but sometimes I wonder if most people just don't feel worth it. Do they feel like this kind of place is where they belong, like the nice places are meant for 'better' people? Heck, I'm the one who always kids around with the whole 'these are my people' jokes when we're in a rough neighborhood."

I think about that for a few seconds. "Yeah, I think that's it exactly. As much as we talk about all the equality and freedom we have, we always revert back to the feudal class system where we all know our place. We've got to have that hierarchy or we just don't feel comfortable, do we?"

"Not to mention that we're supporting some national chain here, instead of supporting a local guy trying to eke out a living. Heck, same thing really. We're giving our money to some big corporation owned by the wigs with money, cuttin' the local workin' stiff like you and me out of another sale."

"Boy, now I'm feeling really good about our decision to eat here . . . "

Erik smiles and nods. "Well hell, so we screwed up again. At least the company's good!" He raises his beer and we bang our mugs together loudly.

As we resume sitting quietly, I realize this is one of the things I like most about Erik—his willingness to be so open about screwing up. Most of us spend our lives justifying the stupid things we do, but Erik embraces them. Not in a way that says he's proud of it, but in a way that says he sees things for what they are. Not an overblown and self-righteous "I've seen the error of my ways and will sin no more" way, but more like, "I know *exactly* how I screw up, and while I'll sure try to improve as time goes by, mostly I need to just be okay with the slow improvements I do make, and not beat myself up over the dumbness around the edges."

Not many of us have the courage and self-confidence to look at life that way. Most of us need to think pretty highly of ourselves, overstating our good sides, justifying the bad stuff. My brother embraces the complete Erik, knowing that beneath both the good decisions and the bad ones is a good man who wants to do good things.

And that's what I love most about him. Well, it's on the list, anyway . . .

CHAIN GUNK

In seed time learn, in harvest teach, in winter enjoy.
William Blake

DAY 23 • OTTAWA, KANSAS TO WARRENSBURG, MISSOURI

Wrapped in warm and humid air the next morning, the first hints of dawn in the sky in front of me, I meander through Ottawa and onto Highway 68 headed east. I find my way through sleepy little towns like Louisburg in Kansas, then Harrisonville in Missouri after crossing the state line, as they begin their days. I stop at a little convenience store in Harrisonville. I've got a route mapped into my Garmin, but I remember that it involves roads that appear pretty iffy on the map—like they might be dirt or gravel roads. Gravel roads on a road bike just aren't pleasant.

I figure that local folks who make the drive to Warrensburg will probably know good back roads to take, so I strike up a conversation with the young couple who run the place, hoping for confirmation that my route is a paved one.

"I'm headed to Warrensburg and wondering if there are some county roads headed east that will get me there?"

The fella looks over at the gal with a puzzled look on his face, then looks back at me and responds. "There might be, but the way to Warrensburg is to follow Highway 7 up to Highway 50 and follow that across."

"Yeah, but since I'm on a bicycle, I'm trying to stay off the busy highways."

They look at each other again, and it's clear they don't understand why a person wouldn't just follow the easy route. "I really don't know any other way to get there. Just follow 7 up to 50 and go across." While he's talking, the gal is looking out the window at my bicycle. She chimes in.

"Wait, you're riding your bicycle all the way to Warrensburg?"

Ah, I feel better now, she's getting the idea. "Right, so I try to stay on the backroads when I can."

"Man, you're getting kind of a late start, aren't you?" the fella asks.

"Well I started the day in Ottawa, so I'm about halfway through my day."

The odd look from before has become one of bewilderment now. He looks back down the road as if he could see Ottawa from here, then looks back at me. A broad smile cuts across his face, accompanied by a quizzical look, evaluating whether or not I'm pulling his leg. "Really?" he says with emphasis.

"Yep. Riding across the country, averaging about 100 miles a day, and today should be right at 100 miles." These little encounters make me feel like Superman. I'm just getting on the bike and riding, probably having a lot more fun than he is today, but he's looking at me like I'm a superhero.

Our conversation shifts to talk about the trip and about cycling, and it's clear to me that they're not likely to be much help with the route. We have good conversation though, and they seem like really great people. After 20 or 30 minutes of chatting, I'm back in the saddle and headed east out of town, enjoying deserted secondary roads for quite a few miles. There comes a point, though, where I'm faced with a fork in the road that takes me either the wrong way or onto gravel.

I opt for the gravel, hoping that it won't last long before dropping me back onto some pavement. Unfortunately, it lasts for five or ten miles.

Gravel can be a lot of fun if you're on a bike made for gravel. Nothing about my road bike with skinny tires is made for gravel. Not to mention the few extra pounds of gear riding up high, raising my center of balance even further. On top of it all, my personality is no stranger to OCD tendencies, and riding along on dirty gravel—kicking up dust and grime into my chain with every spin of the crank—sets my whole being on edge.

While I'm on the gravel, I'm cursing myself a bit. Why not just stick to the major roads, rather than taking the chance on these backroads that so often turn to gravel? The cursing continues as long as the gravel holds out, but once I'm back on smooth pavement I get a bit philosophical about the whole thing. It's a great metaphor for life, isn't it? Stick to the big roads with all the people, and things will probably be smoother. Sure, it'll be more crowded, and a whole lot more monotonous, but you're likely to have fewer bumpy rides, and a lot less gunk on your chain.

But you'll miss the adventure. And sometimes the bumpy road is the one the universe has put in front of you. It's the one that needs taking right now.

Rolling into Warrensburg, I enjoy the nice *old towny* feel of this quaint college town. I notice a bike shop as I roll past, and I decide to stop for a little adjusting. Okay, so a little adjusting *and* a little chain cleaning . . .

It's early in the day still, and I love finding local bike shops in the towns I ride through. I feel good giving them a little business, and I love meeting and visiting with local folks who are cyclists. Rolling through the front door of the bike shop, I realize that the real reason for stopping here probably has more to do with my desire for conversation with other cyclists than it does with my bike's need for any adjustment, which I could do myself anyway.

But there is all that new gunk on the chain . . .

Leaning my bike up against a counter, I wander back toward the shop area, where the mechanic is working on a bike. I love that about small local bike shops—there's usually just a single employee in the store, who is both the mechanic and the sales clerk. They're rarely good at both, so I need to size up whether this fella is mostly sales clerk or mostly mechanic. Jeremy is the young fella's name, and the fact that he's pretty much ignoring me as I wander through the shop gives me a nice warm feeling. Mostly mechanic. I like that.

But the other two fellas back there with him come right out to greet me and chat. "You ridin' your bike across the country?" one of them asks.

A bit surprised, I say that yes, I am. Sure I have a little pack on the back of my bike, but it's small, and just because I'm touring, why do they guess that?

We chat, and it turns out these two fellas are also riding their bikes across the country. They're doing it all in one summer, and we just happen to meet up here in Warrensburg. Cool.

We exchange stories about routes and gear. This is what cross-country cyclists always want to talk with each other about first—routes and gear. Which route did you take across the desert southwest? Where did you cross the divide? What route are you planning over the Appalachians? Where will you end up? Is this all your gear? Really?

James and Lei are from "out east." Lei is from New York City, and James is from Buffalo. They're both young fellas, probably in their 20s, out on the adventure of a lifetime. James has taken this adventure quest to a whole new level. He's never really ridden a bike. Maybe once or twice, but never owned a bike and ridden regularly. I'm stunned. I didn't imagine such a thing possible—to grow up in America and not learn to ride a bike. Just goes to show how limited my perspective is. But

James's friend Lei suggested this cross-country adventure, and James thought it was a good idea, so he ordered a bike and had it shipped directly to their starting point in California. He flew out to California, met his bike for the first time, strapped on touring gear, climbed into the saddle, and started to ride.

Really.

Can you imagine such a thing? Strapping touring gear on a bike, climbing on, and learning to ride? I train *extensively* to do these long rides, worrying endlessly about whether I'm at a high enough level of fitness, or whether I'm calloused enough in the nether regions to avoid saddle sores. This young punk barely knows the front of a bike from the back, but just climbs on, and starts riding across the country!

The gall.

Well that, and a lot of courage. Sure, it'd be easy to use words like silly or dumb rather than courageous, and while there's undoubtedly a bit of silly and dumb in what James is doing, there's also a huge dose of courage required to make it happen. Was it an old Apple commercial that said something like the impossible can only be done by those who don't know it's impossible?

JEREMY AT THE BIKE SHOP

Wherever you go, go with all your heart.

Confucius

Most of the fellow cross-country cyclists I meet along this trip
are young people. In their 20s, probably at a point of transition
in life. Maybe they've just graduated from college, or they're
moving from one relationship to another in life, searching for
"the one." It's a time in life full of passage and metamorphosis.

James and Lei are talking excitedly with each other and
with Jeremy. They're not really seeing this as a passage or a
transition. They just see it as adventure, and this was the right
time to do it. I realize that it's the spirit of adventure that we
always feel from fellow sojourners, not some spirit of transition.

Are we more likely to reach for adventure during times
of transition in life? Does the transition become our excuse or
our permission to reach out for adventure, like a last hurrah
before we fling ourselves back into the arms of safety and fa-
miliarity? Maybe transition is a gateway emotion to adventure.

Nosing around the bike shop, I feel the excitement bub-
bling out of James and Lei. When this ride is over, will they draw
that blanket of security around themselves in life, drowning in

what they already know, saving adventure for the next great transition in their lives? Will I? What do I need to do in order to nourish adventure from the way I live my life day to day?

With one hand we reach for adventure, with the other we cling to comforts into which we settle. Is this bad? Should the side of us that clings to comfort feel guilty about the song we hear calling us to adventure? Should the adventure seeker within us scorn the comfort lover? I'm sure we've all got a different "balance" that we seek between comfort and adventure, and I'm learning more and more how important it is for me to find that point of balance.

I envy people who have jobs they love, where they find that right balance of comfort and adventure. They love going to work in the morning and feel great about themselves when they get back home. While I envy them, I also realize that I don't know very many of them.

Even more, I envy people who have found that perfect balance of comfort and adventure in their marriage. I'm hardly one to pontificate on what it takes to make a relationship work, but I know that it's hard to discover that balance, and build it into the day-to-day interactions that become the habits in a relationship.

There's a kind of comfort that can come from something that's very long-term. It's a comfort we can't find anywhere else. Whether it's a job we hold for 20 years or 40 years, or a marriage that lasts a whole lifetime, I'm beginning to see and feel the gap in our lives that happens when we don't have that deep and long-lasting ground wire.

How many people find that balance, I wonder? Life-long relationships to fill their memory and soothe their soul, side-by-side with a spirit overflowing with adventure. I look into the back of the bicycle shop and see James and Lei laughing and talking excitedly with Jeremy, and wonder if any of them will find that balance in life. Will they have the courage to continue to fling themselves into adventure, even after finding the contentment of constancy? Will they be willing to embrace the suffering that sometimes accompanies adventure, while also the comfort of stability? For that matter, will they find the courage to maintain and feed stability?

It turns out that James (the one with the gall to launch himself into this adventure with essentially no training and no cycling experience) did, in fact, develop some pretty significant saddle sores on the trip. He did suffer quite a bit gaining the fitness he needed. But, in the end, the invincible spirit and recuperative abilities of youth carried the day. I send a silent wish toward both of them, hoping they learn a way to discover the balance better than I have.

Jeremy finishes up on Lei's bike, and we three riders exchange good-byes and good lucks, may the force be with you, and all that. It's a very exciting ritual I've discovered with fellow travelers, this "may the force be with you" moment as we part ways. Those might not be the words exchanged, but it's the sentiment. It started way back in Monterey, on the first day of my journey, with a young woman I met at the airport who was on a journey of transition herself. I've felt it over and over with fellow vagabonds, and for whatever reason, find the ritual uplifting and exciting.

Jeremy turns his attention to my bike, and we chat about my trip and about Jeremy's life. I tell Jeremy about the blogging I do, and he asks for my website address so he can get his folks to check it out. They've been married for 30 years, and he feels like they've descended into an unhealthy comfort zone, one where they don't get out and do exciting things. He figures maybe seeing someone their own age having adventures like this will motivate them to get out and find a little something active in life.

That balance again. Learning how to enjoy comfort, without languishing in it. Learning how to embrace adventure, without letting it destroy contentment.

THE SUNRISE CAFE

*The best portion of a good man's life—his little,
nameless, unremembered acts of kindness and love.*

William Wordsworth

DAY 24 • WARRENSBURG TO HARTSBURG, MISSOURI

The predawn air drips with moisture as I roll out of my hotel in Warrensburg. It's a warm wetness, not quite rain, but a heavy mist that keeps the pavement wet and me soaked as I venture out onto US 50 headed east.

My expectation this morning is for a decent road, a good shoulder, and reasonably light traffic. I built this expectation before starting the trip by talking to a local cyclist in Sedalia on the phone. "Decent," "good," and "reasonable" are not the words coming to mind as I wade through the mist along a highway packed solid with two eastbound lanes of people driving fast. The blinking lights I have on my back do little to assuage my fear of the traffic roaring past me through the foggy mist and predawn poor visibility, so I stay as far to the right as I can on the shoulder—even though this means I'm riding through all sorts of glass and other junk strewn along the pavement, most of it invisible to me in the poor light.

This is the downside of shoulders for bicycles. Shoulders are a magnet for the glass, pieces of metal, and all the other detritus of our motorized culture. These things aren't a problem for modern-day car and truck tires, but for lightweight cycling tires they're brutal.

Predictably, after 10 or 15 miles, I'm standing on the side of the road changing a flat tire, drenched from the spray of passing cars. Interestingly, a young woman (thirty-something) pulls off the road to ask if I need help. Nice. That's a pretty unusual gesture—for someone in a car to pull off to ask a cyclist if they need help. Beyond that, for a young woman to do so is a measure of concern for a fellow human that I find very heartwarming in the twilight mist.

Fifteen minutes and a new tube later, I'm off and running (or rolling) down the road. The sun's peeked through some eastern clouds, and the mist has stopped. The traffic volume has slowed down a bit, so I feel more comfortable staying out on the edge of the shoulder, where I can avoid some of the sharp stuff. The kindness and concern demonstrated by the woman along the road has buoyed my spirits, and I'm ready for breakfast by the time I'm rolling through the back streets of Sedalia.

Spotting a little dive called the Sunrise Cafe, I pull over and lean my bike against the front window. It's a tiny little diner in a working-class section of town. My kind of place.

Walking in the front door, I'm greeted by air heavy with cigarette smoke. It takes me by such surprise that I just stand there for a minute, looking at a couple who are both smoking as they drink coffee. Missouri must be one of the few states that hasn't outlawed smoking in restaurants yet. In that instant, standing there engulfed in smoke and staring at folks who are staring back at me, I realize that I'm likely to encounter a lot of this from here to the east coast, so I might as well buck up and accept it.

Once we all move past the awkward moment where the weird old dripping-wet guy in spandex and blinking lights who's standing just inside the front door is gazing around at all the people who are gazing back at him, I sit down and make myself at home. Everyone goes back to what they were doing. *These aren't the droids you're looking for.*

The waitress seems really concerned that I need a big breakfast, so she brings me two plates stacked high with food that could easily feed five people. I eat about half of it (that's enough for two or three people), and she wonders if it isn't good, since I didn't eat it all. No, I assure her, it was wonderful. Then I look around, and notice that I probably weigh half of what anyone else in the place weighs.

I'm a pretty adaptable fella, able to fit into most crowds and be neighborly with just about anyone. I realize that here in the middle of Missouri, I'm beginning to experience a cultural shift that I need to become okay with. From here to Annapolis, folks are generally going to be heavier, and smoking will be far more common than it was across the west.

Not a slam, not an unfounded stereotype, just an observation. Just sayin' . . .

I enjoy several great conversations with some really good folks at the Sunrise Cafe, taking my time and savoring the good company. My belly full of good food, my soul replenished by communion with good people, I head back out into a morning now filled with sunlight.

THE KATY TRAIL

The woods are lovely, dark and deep. But I have promises to keep, and miles to go before I sleep.

Robert Frost

St. Charles, MO

Sedalia, MO

DAN AND SUSAN

*Why are there trees I never walk under but large
and melodious thoughts descend upon me?*
Walt Whitman, *Song of the Open Road*

I meander a bit through Sedalia, searching for the place to hop
onto the Katy Trail headed east. Through town, the trail actually follows streets that aren't always well marked. Maybe it's
just that I'm not always on the right streets, which is probably
more likely. I find the trail on the northeast side of town, which
I'll follow from here to Illinois.

The Katy is a *rail trail,* or a trail built on the old rail bed
of an abandoned railway. The Katy (like most of these trails)
is paved with crusher fines, which is finely crushed rock that
packs into a hard surface. The surface works great for mountain bikes, and so long as it's dry, works fine for road tires as
well. The trail has no perceptible grade and the dry surface is
dandy for me as I leave the pavement behind and begin my
sail along one of the great treasures of our nation.

I've left traffic behind me, and I feel a big smile stretching
my face. I'm gliding through lush forest, listening to the birds

and frogs around me, enjoying bucolic scenery float past me.
Now and then I pass a fellow traveler, though I don't stop to
talk. The stark change from the deadly traffic and noise along
Highway 50 this morning to the pastoral beauty and quiet
along this trail makes me wonder what it would take for our
country to embrace the thousands of miles of wasted and
abandoned railroad right of ways that are sitting idle and turn
them into a national string of jewels, creating a bicycle route
stretching across the nation.

I can't imagine many places as enjoyable to ride a bicycle
as the Katy Trail. The only sounds are the soft crunching of
my tires on the path and a gentle rustle of the leaves. Ahead
of me, the trail is a ribbon winding through a tunnel of arched
branches beneath the forest surrounding the trail. Now and
then, one side or the other of the trail will reveal a few hundred yards of gap in the forest, and the surrounding farmland
will leak right up to the edge of the path.

At some point, I miss a shift and my chain climbs up onto
my spokes, stripping a couple of them from the drive side of my
back wheel. While I carry tools to fix most things that might go
wrong with the bike, I don't carry the right tools to fix drive-
side spokes, so this little problem consumes a good part of my
day. I walk the bike for several miles along the path, and while
I'm frustrated at the delay, the walk is lovely, and I get to meet
and talk to several cyclists who stop and ask if they can help.

Of course they can't help, not unless they happen to have
a chain whip so I can pull my cassette and access those spokes,
but the gesture warms my heart each time it happens. There it
is again—concern for the fellow traveler on the road.

At one point, a couple riding a tandem comes up, riding
the same direction I'm walking.

"Looks like a lot of trouble," the fella says as he coasts
to a stop beside me.

"Yep. A drive-side spoke. You don't happen to carry a
chain whip, do you?"

"Sorry, but we don't. How will you get that fixed?"

"I'll cross a road eventually and get a ride back to Sedalia to a bike shop."

"I'm Dan," he smiles warmly as he reaches his hand toward me. "And this is my wife, Susan."

I introduce myself while shaking hands, then point up the trail. "Hey I don't want to hold you guys up, but thanks for stopping."

"You're not holding us up," Dan replies. "We're making our way across the trail doing 30 to 50 miles a day, and hope for as many distractions as possible as we go." He looks back at Susan, and with a nod between them they start the tandem slowly rolling forward as I start to walk. They maintain my walking speed with me, riding and chatting.

We talk through the introductory pleasantries, ride details and all that. I learn that they've taken a week off work and are riding the trail together on their tandem. He's close to retirement, while she might be a few years younger than he is. He works for an airline as a pilot, and she has some sort of online hobby/business.

"So how long have you been flying planes, Dan?" I ask.

"Over 45 years. Been with this same airline for nearly 40 years."

"That's a rarity these days—working for one company your whole career, I mean."

He smiles as he nods. "They've treated me well."

"And you've treated them well, too!" Susan chimes in. "It takes two to make that tango work in the long run, and you've given them a lot, Dan."

There's no bite or resentment in her tone, just love and encouragement. A supportive partner not letting her mate sell himself short.

"I wonder why it's so rare today," I muse as we make our way down the path, warm autumn air rustling leaves around us now and then. "I wonder how come people don't stick with companies for a lifetime anymore, and why companies treat people like commodities."

Susan shrugs slightly, "I think it's because we've become so focused on the short term, and we ignore the long term and the big picture. In everything really. We don't *invest* anymore. Companies view people as short-term assets, and people view companies in a very mercenary way. Everybody is in it for themselves and for what they can get out of the deal right now. It's about what I can barter, trade, or take from this relationship right now, never about how I can invest in our joint venture so it returns more in the long run."

She looks past me at a picturesque farmstead beyond the trees that line the trail here. The wheels of their tandem crackle along the surface beneath, my footsteps crunching a rhythm as we progress in silence for a few minutes. Her eyes have a faraway look, a very slight smile on her lips.

Dan picks up on the sentiment Susan began. "Here we are in Mark Twain country, and his quote about money comes to mind. I don't remember the exact words, but something about money being like manure—for it to do any good you have to spread it around. I know the quote is about money, but it really applies to everything we invest—money, time, energy."

Susan turns back toward the road ahead, smiling at the comment, focus back on the conversation. She sets her wrist on Dan's shoulder and points ahead to where sunlight filters through the trees in a particularly pretty way. I've never thought much about tandem cycling, but watching Dan and Susan, I find myself reflecting across our conversation, tandem cycling, and relationships.

The front rider (*captain* in tandem speak) has to spend a little more focus than normal on the steering and balance, since he's handling twice the bike, while the back rider (*stoker* in tandem speak) is free to take in more of the surroundings than a rider normally would. The stoker has to trust the captain completely, and the captain has to accept the additional responsibility for keeping the team upright. With that additional work and responsibility, the captain has to stay more focused on the driving and so will miss much of the scenery the team is riding through.

Which is where the stoker comes in. While not oblivious to the riding, the stoker is responsible for soaking in more of the scenery and sharing with the captain who would probably have missed it. Teammates, each with a different focus, neither ignoring the other, both focused on the shared experience. Teamwork. Making the team work. Investing.

A squirrel chatters loudly at us as we pass too closely to where he's sitting in a tree. The distant sound of a train whistle drifts through the trees to us. Hearing a distant sound brings the quiet around the trail into focus. Hearing things from far away only happens when it's not too noisy close by.

"So how long have you two been married?" I ask.

"Seven years," Dan answers. "This trip is kind of an anniversary celebration for us."

"It's a second marriage for both of us," Susan adds.

"Darn," I answer with a smile. "I was hoping you were going to tell me you'd been married for 40 years or something. That would prove out the whole *investing in relationships* notion."

Dan smiles before answering. "We were both married to other people for decades, both raised families. We both ended up at the end of the relationship looking at our partners, realizing we hadn't invested in each other or in the relationship. In the end, we'd just drained too much and invested too little."

After a brief silence, Susan finishes the thought. "So, we're committed to making this relationship about investing instead of taking."

Clearly, this is something they've thought about and are committed to. Based on my brief interaction with them, they're obviously happy, so maybe they're getting it figured out. After a few minutes of silence, Dan says, "Well darlin', shall we get on up the trail?"

"Sure. It's been great chatting with you Neil. Best of luck getting those spokes fixed."

Dan and Susan roll away up the trail, leaving me in deep thought about the nature of making a relationship work, whether it's a job or a marriage. I lament the state of things, yet I'm no different from everyone else in this regard. I'm divorced, and I've worked for several different companies throughout my career. How much investing have I done in the relationships in my life, and how much have I treated each one like a short game?

I look up the trail at Dan and Susan as they fade further from me up the trail. He's focused on the trail ahead, keeping them upright and safe, while she's watching intently all around for bits and pieces of the world to share with him. Just before they round a corner, she points off to the left excitedly, and I wonder what unexpected slice of the universe she just brought into his life. You can feel the investment they continue to make in each other after seven years of marriage.

The tiniest of breezes brushes against my cheek and rustles the leaves along the side of the trail. The silence wraps around me again as Dan and Susan have disappeared. Sunlight dapples the arched canopy through which the trail meanders.

CATS

Of all God's creatures, there is only one that cannot be made slave of the lash. That one is the cat. If man could be crossed with the cat it would improve man, but it would deteriorate the cat.

Mark Twain

Hartsburg is a tiny town along the Katy Trail. Making my way to the front door of the Globe Hotel Bed and Breakfast, I step over a couple of cats who lounge in the warm afternoon in a way that only cats can lounge. This is their porch, and they have complete confidence that those who enter will give them space and respect, as the universe has deemed right and good. Upon entering the front door, two additional cats scatter quickly into the parlor to my left, while another spills lazily over the edges of a bookshelf in the front hall.

This is the home of a cat person.

I'm not a cat person. It's not that I dislike cats, I just don't have any particular affinity for them. In college, I had a cat that I was very attached to. The cat's name was Bonnie, and she was Siamese. Positively overflowing with personality, she was also very much a "one person" cat. She had kittens in my closet before I got her spayed, and every night after I went to bed she'd drag her kittens up into my bed one by one, depositing them under the covers down around my legs, and leave them for me to babysit while she caroused around the house all night. Before dawn in the morning, she'd come retrieve them from me, and put them back in the closet, where she'd take care of them all day.

My friend Rick came to town to visit one weekend. At the breakfast table, Bonnie meandered through life as usual, meaning that she jumped up on the table, where she knew I'd share my breakfast with her. Rick was sitting at the table, and he assumed that a cat jumping up onto the breakfast table represented extremely poor manners on the part of the cat. He summarily swept Bonnie from the table, and she landed indignantly several feet away on the floor. She glared up at him, fixing his image in her little cat brain. Remembering.

About a year later, Rick came visiting again. He meandered up the rickety back stairs of the old house where I lived, and along the narrow hallway that led to my apartment. He knocked once and let himself in, announcing his arrival as he came through the door. I was sitting at the kitchen table studying, while Bonnie was curled up on the other side of the table. Her head came up as the door opened, alert for any abnormality in her world.

Bonnie heard Rick's voice, looked carefully at his face for about three seconds, then bounded off the table toward him, wrapping her paws around his lower leg, digging her claws deeply into his flesh, sinking her teeth repeatedly into his calf muscle. Rick danced on one leg impressively, attempting to shake his attacker from his leg, while making increasingly disturbing sounds of shock and indignation.

After inflicting what she deemed to be the appropriate dose of retribution, Bonnie jumped aside, leapt back up onto the kitchen table, and began licking her paws. Rick stared at his bloody leg. My mouth hung open in shock. It was the only time in Bonnie's life that she was ever mean to any person.

While I don't know much about cats, I do know that they have memories. And that they understand the concept of retribution.

Here at the Globe Hotel, it's Rick I'm meeting. I smile at the fortuity of the situation as Rick stands from the chair in the dining room to cross the room and embrace me, a cat jumping from his lap as he does. A tiny little spoke of memory and irony touches me, reaching out from the hub of the past into the wheel of here and now.

Rick and I will be riding together on the trail for the next couple of days. We're a motley collection of widely varying cycling gear and competencies, and I'm looking forward to a couple of days of a social and leisurely pace along the trail.

Jeannette, the proprietor at the Globe, has been out in the back garden with other guests and wanders through the back door, the cats all alert and attentive as the Only Human Who Matters walks into their domain and makes her way through the house. Jeannette is a woman small in physical stature and large in personal presence. She carries the evidence of long-earned wisdom well, simultaneously friendly and in-command in a way that only small older women can be. She shows us to our respective rooms, cats scattering in front of us as we climb the old stairs to the second floor.

"And this is your room," she says to me as she opens the door, pushing a cat aside who clearly thinks it's his room. "And remember, you have to keep the door closed because cats aren't allowed in the guest rooms."

I smile and chuckle, assuming she's joking with me. Cats are dripping from every corner of the house; how can they not be allowed in the guest rooms? She sees the look of confusion on my face, and continues. "No really. I don't want them in the guest rooms. They might get stuck in there, and not everyone loves cats, you know. I don't want someone to be forced to deal with a cat if they don't want to."

I measure my response, not wanting to sound disrespect-ful, but also truly curious. "But if they didn't want to deal with cats, they wouldn't be staying here, would they?"

Jeannette's patronizing smile has only a hint of reproach at such a silly question, and it's clear that she's accustomed to dealing with dullards such as myself who ask such arcane ques-tions. I'm only a tiny bit offended by the look. She must sense this, because she leans toward me, taking my right forearm in her left hand. She's probably a full foot shorter than I am, and she pats my forearm with her right hand gently. The smile on her face evolves from patronizing to a full ten thousand watt beacon of loving acceptance. She bounces her forehead lightly off my upper arm in one last gesture of affection, then turns and starts herding cats down the stairs in front of her.

As she carefully negotiates the steps to avoid the cats weaving beneath her step, I watch after her, wanting desper-ately to go help her, but realizing that this is her home, and she must negotiate this descent many times a day on her own. Looking down to my feet, I notice two cats watching her go. They feel my gaze on them, and look up at me in a way that says, very clearly, "It's okay, we let her think that we're not allowed in the room."

Opening the door, I step in with my gear, the cats march-ing in beneath my feet. As I turn to close my door, Rick's door across the hall opens briefly, a cat tossed unceremoniously into the hall. Rick notices me watching and smiles.

"Never learned your lesson, did you?" I ask.

He gives me a "pshaw" look before turning back into his room. After the door closes, the cat looks at me in a way that asks, very clearly, "You're not with him, right? Because I'm re-membering him, and you don't want to be part of that memory."

PLEASE

*Better to remain silent and be thought a fool
than to speak out and remove all doubt.*

Often ascribed to **Abraham Lincoln**

After cleaning up, we head out and find supper. Hartsburg is a
tiny little town, and I have to assume that Katy Trail users add
significantly to the economy here. There's enough commerce
coming into town to support a couple of different inns, so I
assume this must also indicate potential for other "support"
dollars, like dining customers. We wander around the little
burg to see what there is to eat. Actually, "wander around" is
a bit of an overstatement; you can stand in the street and see
the whole town.

The only open place we can see is the local bar, which
doesn't bother us a bit since the thing we really want is normally found at a bar. Wandering through the front door, we
find a seat at a high-top table, learning quickly to deal with the
haze from cigarette smoke around us. There's nobody really
waiting tables, just a kid behind the bar trying to keep up. I
walk up to the bar to find out about the food menu.

"It's Thursday," he informs me.

"Right," I respond.

Then I wait. I know from the way he's looking at me that there's something significant about his statement, but I haven't figured it out yet. He wanders down to the end of the bar to grab another Bud Light for a patron.

Eventually he wanders back to me. "So, wadya have?"

"I think we want a couple of beers, but what we really want is food. Do you have a kitchen?"

"It's Thursday."

Well, this is an interesting conversational circle we seem to be stuck in. "Right. But what does that mean? Do you not serve food on Thursday?"

He nods. I'm not sure if the nod means, "Yes we do serve food on Thursday" or "Yes we don't serve food on Thursday." I'm at a bit of a loss, and probably have a slack-jawed look to me as I try to figure a way to ease into some level of understanding. A particularly dense cloud of cigarette smoke drifts between me and the bartender, coming from the guy leaning against the bar beside me. He steps in to help out.

"Town kinda shuts down on Thursdays. Kitchen is shut down here. The other place in town that serves food shuts down Thursdays, too."

Aha! Now I get it. Progress. "Ah. Okay. So is there maybe a store in town where I can buy something to warm up?"

The bartender gives his head a little shake and his shoulders a little shrug, seemingly confused that I still don't understand. "Well I can warm ya up a frozen pizza."

It all seems surreal to me, like I'm not speaking the right language. The guy next to me adds that there are no stores open in town. It's Thursday. Everybody closes down. Except the bar here.

Looking back at the bartender, I confirm what I think I understand. "So it's Thursday, and you don't serve food, but you can heat us up a frozen pizza. Right?"

"Yep." He seems relieved that I finally understand. I order

some pizza for us, even though it's Thursday, along with some longnecks.

The conversation reminds me of a comical exchange I had at a Burger King when I first moved to Cincinnati back in the eighties. As preamble, it's helpful to understand that in Cincinnati, one of their unique language usages is that the word "please" means "I'm sorry, I didn't hear you, can you please repeat what you just said?" I had just moved there, and didn't realize this. To me, using the word "please" by itself meant "yes, please."

When my turn came to order, I stepped up to the counter. "I'll have a Whopper and a Diet Coke, please."

The clerk hit a few buttons, and repeated the order as trained. "A Whopper and a Diet Coke. Is that correct?"

"Please."

Taking my apparent faulty hearing in stride, she repeated, only slightly louder this time, "That'll be a Whopper and a Diet Coke. Is that correct?"

Not sure if she's just distracted and didn't notice me respond the first time, I respond again, this time making sure she's looking at me and listening. "Please."

Thinking she had a doozy on her hands with really bad hearing, she leaned toward me, just to be sure I could hear her. Quite loudly, she repeated again, "You want a Whopper and a Diet Coke, right?"

Is she just making fun of me? I wondered. I looked around, wondering if someone was filming this, having a good time with a practical joke. But everyone close by was looking at me like I was being mean to this poor little high school girl. I leaned back toward her—our faces were only a foot or two apart at this point—and said in the most clear and loud voice that I could, "Please."

I was both deaf and very slow on the uptake, or at least that's what she must have been thinking. Everyone around us was watching, and I couldn't get over the feeling that they were about to call the police on me. What the heck was I doing wrong? Using the same very loud voice, she repeated again, annunciating each of the words very slowly, "You. Want. A. Whopper. And. A. Diet. Coke . . . Is. That. Right?"

I was at my wit's end, and was about to just turn around and leave, when the guy behind me smiled and stepped in. "Yes ma'am, you have his order right."

She was looking at me with pity, I guess figuring that guy was my handler and was letting me try to order by myself this time, and I screwed it up. Again. I paid her, and thanked her, then turned to the guy who helped me, a look of bewilderment on my face.

"Not from around here, are you?" He went on to explain briefly what the word *"please"* meant in Cincinnatian.

"No I'm not. And thank you! Wait, what does *thank you* mean in Cincinnati speak?"

JEANNETTE

The language of friendship is not words but meanings.
Henry David Thoreau

Back at our high-top table, we share a good chuckle at the inadequacies of language. We have fun with stories about Hartsburg, but settle quickly into conversations about our lives. It's good to spend time catching up on children who have grown up, careers and relationships that have evolved, and the other little slices of the life we've seen as we've moved through it.

Rick is one of my oldest friends in the world. We've been friends since we were nine or ten years old, when we lived a couple of houses away from each other. He and I had one of those friendships that orbited around the other things happening in our respective lives. We never really hung out in the same crowds, or did the same things, but we always maintained our friendship.

We haven't seen each other in years, and I find great comfort in the ease with which our conversation slips back into very familiar territory. I reflect back on my earlier conversation today with Dan and Susan, and the concept of investing in relationships. How have Rick and I stayed friends through the years, when we haven't really invested in each other in any way? Dan and Susan are committed to building a relationship based on mutual investment because they know this is required to make it last, yet here I sit with an old friend whom I've invested nothing significant in, and we're laughing and joking and having a great time.

Balance, maybe. Maybe Rick and I stay friends because we don't ask much of each other. We're just a couple of old friends who enjoy company with each other now and then. The investment we make is just a little shared time now and then. Listen to each other's stories. Buy a beer. Be a friend.

Investing comes in many shapes and forms, I realize as our conversation rolls along. Rick and I are both introverts, and our communication styles mesh nicely. Long periods of quiet work fine with us, and much is generally said with just a few words. The relationship doesn't demand great depth, just consistency. Later in the evening, lying awake in bed, listening to cats moving around the house, I come to realize that the term *investing style* has meaning both in the financial world and the world of relationships.

Breakfast the next morning is a very social affair at the Globe. Jeannette had invited us to sit with her in the living room last night to visit, but we migrated to bed instead, since we had an expectation of an early start in the morning. However, when morning comes, it's clear that Jeanette holds all the schedule cards, and an early start isn't part of the hand we've been dealt.

Which is okay. I reset my expectations, and settle down to enjoy breakfast with friends new and old. Jeanette shares her story with us as we share the breakfast on the table, and I'm surprised at the candor and detail she includes in the story as she tells it.

Not that Jeannette's story is shocking. It includes only the normal amount of scandal—no more than everyone else's stories. It's just a life story told by someone who's lived her days fully and with passion. Yet, for some reason, it feels almost uncomfortable to me as I listen.

But Jeannette doesn't seem uncomfortable at all. Her story ranges, ebbs, and flows as the breakfast on the table disappears. Observing, I realize that the thing that has me uncomfortable is her deep sense of honesty and her unabashed frankness. She's someone who's seen life from a lot of perspectives, and is sharing some of those perspectives in a strikingly genuine way.

Putting myself in Jeanette's shoes, it's easy to imagine that running a place like this could become a significant part of your social interaction. Meeting new people every day, most of whom you'll never see again, sharing your story with them and hearing theirs. I don't get the impression that Jeanette is a lonely person at all—quite the opposite. She seems to be in a very full and happy place in life. Maybe it's her confidence in her place in life right now that makes her feel so open to share her story with others.

Whatever the reason, what's very clear to me is that Jeannette's investing style regarding relationships is dramatically different from mine. Yesterday we were complete strangers, and a week from now she may barely remember us, yet she's pouring her soul out to us over toast and jam at the breakfast table.

I'm not that confident. I'll say "Pass the toast please," and tell a fun little anecdote, the socially correct mix of humor and truth. But in terms of sharing deep parts of me, that's just not my style. Not until we know each other much better. We'll share little bits, getting a little deeper each time, then over a long period of time we will have dug deeply into each other's story, together, jointly, in concert. Each of us sharing equally in the digging.

If I find myself doing most of the digging, and find that I'm the only one going deeply, then I'll stop, and we'll stay shallow. But not Jeannette. Jeannette is courageous in a way I admire. She charges forward, all engines ahead. Whether or not you choose to ride along is your decision completely, but that isn't going to impact her head of steam.

Jeannette goes for broke. Her fearlessness can likely create a wealth of deep relationships over a lifetime. I watch her as she speaks, and applaud her audacious style while recognizing the flaw in my own personality.

A leisurely breakfast while listening to Jeanette might be different from our expectation, but it's a perfect start to these next two days of friendship and social reconnection along the Katy Trail. Taking time with a new stranger who's walked into your life, getting to know them, listening to their story.

No hurry. Laid back. Very social. Telling your story, listening to someone's story. Investing.

NOTE: *All things change, and as-of the writing of this story, The Globe Hotel has changed as well. Jeannette is no longer the proprietor, and the new owners have a strict "no pets" policy. Guests today will miss the feline ambiance that Rick and I experienced. But then, I'm not really a cat person. Neither is Rick. It goes without saying that most cats probably aren't really "Rick felines" either.*

GAME DAY

The leaves of memory seemed to make
A mournful rustling in the dark.

Henry Wadsworth Longfellow

DAY 25 • HARTSBURG TO RHINELAND, MISSOURI

Riding on the Katy Trail is a very convivial undertaking. Yesterday, before Hartsburg, I was pounding hard down the trail, eventually missing a shift, breaking spokes, slowing me down. The slower pace let me meet Dan and Susan. Riding along at a very leisurely pace this morning, I'm coming to understand a complexion to the Katy Trail that I could easily have missed.

It's social. Very social. Everybody I meet along the trail seems to be riding as a social endeavor. There are a couple of gals about my age whom I stop and talk to for 15 minutes at one point. They spend their vacations traveling to different rail-trails around the country. Among the rail trail enthusiast crowd, the Katy is a very big deal, and Janice and Susan have looked forward to this trip for a long time. They're from the South, just a couple of gals who enjoy riding their bikes, combining vacation time with the enjoyment of beautiful places like the Katy, investing in the friendship they have with one another.

Today, a Friday, we run into several groups of people riding toward Columbia, home of the Mizzou—that's the University of Missouri—Tigers. Mizzou has a home game tomorrow, and there are those who like to turn the game into a pilgrimage that involves bike riding along the trail, spending the night before the game in town, and making a real weekend of it. The logistics vary a bit from group to group, but the shared elements seem to be beer, bonding, and Mizzou football.

Another common theme is the notion of *through biking*, meaning traveling from one end of the trail to the other. Some folks camp, some folks stay in bed-and-breakfasts, some folks mix it up a bit. But all the folks I talk to are spending about a week making the pilgrimage across the state, riding something like 50 miles a day, meeting folks along the way, enjoying the beauty of the trail, enjoying the ride.

I like this social pace. My entire trip to date has revolved around significant daily pedaling. I've taken a couple of rest days, but aside from that, the really easy days were 60 or 70 miles. These next couple of days will only cover 25 or 30 miles each day, allowing lots of time for meeting, visiting, and easy pedaling. The social pace encourages easy conversation, and Rick and I have several chances to talk as we ride, letting me appreciate this time with my old friend in ways I couldn't have otherwise.

Our day ends in Rhineland, guests of Amanda who runs The Doll House Bed and Breakfast. After we clean up, we make our way over to the Trailside Bar and Grill, where we fill our bellies with decent small-town America good food.

There's a myth in American folklore that small-town food is always good. Maybe it's not just American folklore, it could be that the mythology around small-town living anywhere in the world creates the notion that the food is good. And sometimes it is, but not always. In fact, I'd venture to say that most of the time it isn't. Like anywhere else on earth, it just all depends on the cook.

We love to glamorize the country life. The *Green Acres* mythology is alive and well in most of America, but the reality of life in a small town is rarely anything like the mythology. I suppose we create mythology about the "olden days" of any flavor. Whether it's an actual memory, or a fantasy about *a better time and a better place,* we like to add color and vibrancy to our myths. It helps us imagine the world as we want it to be. Which is sometimes good, sometimes not so good. The good German folks who settled this town of Rhineland back in the 19th century thought the great flat expanse of the flood plain along the Missouri River was a perfect place to build a town. Human history is full of stories about floods, and nobody has kept it a secret that when a flood happens, it happens in a flood plain. But the folks building the town saw the town they wanted to build through their idealized vision, so they built it down in the nice flat flood plain where it was easy.

Then in 1993 reality struck Rhineland when the Missouri River flooded, submerging the town. As it turns out, the folks who lived here were among the first to accept federal funds to move their town up the hill. Picked up homes and everything, and just moved up the hill. Very little is left down on the old flood plain—you can't even see the new town from where the old town sat.

Except The Doll House. The owners decided to say no thanks to the federal dollars, and just stayed where they were. In some places, you can still see the lines halfway up the first floor walls where the flood waters crested in the old house.

Who knows what the "most right" course of action was back in 1993. Most folks said please and thank you to the American taxpayer and moved up the hill, but the folks who owned The Doll House decided they wanted to stick with their version of a beautiful life on the flood plain. So they stayed, and the house sits mostly alone in a beautiful river valley.

After supper, I take a walk before the sun sets, strolling slowly along the old roads where the town once stood. There's a quiet cemetery up on a hill behind a beautiful old Catholic church, from which I watch a stunning midwestern sunset develop. Gazing out across the broad flood plain, the Missouri River looks far away this evening, peaceful and nonthreatening.

I guess our internal vision of the world as we want it to

be is what keeps us going as humans. It gives us those nice bright colors, the greens of summer, the peaceful river rather than the raging flood. It helps us see the sunny day we want in the world. It builds our endlessly hopeful spirit, and that's a good thing overall.

Our dreams become a big part of who we are. We build the relationships in our lives around those dreams. Our jobs, our lovers, and everything that we become grows out of that dream. But pictures can fade over time, and colors can dull. It takes intention and effort to protect them, and hold them, and keep them healthy.

Which takes me back to the conversation I had with Susan and Dan earlier on the trail about relationships in our lives. It's so darned easy to look at a faded photograph and observe how faded it is, and somehow blame the photograph for becoming faded. They fade when we don't take care of them. It's predictable and constant.

Leaning against a tree up in the cemetery, I watch the deep wash of the sunset begin to fill in across the valley. My mind flips through the scrapbook of my life as I watch the vibrant glow expand and glow. I want to learn to keep the colors vibrant, both in my vision of what I hope for in life and my memory of what I cherish.

I notice a good deal of activity at the fairgrounds in town as I make my way back down the hill and to The Doll House. Signs around town advertise a tractor pull the next day, and they're getting the grounds ready for it. There's something primally fun about a tractor pull, hooking a chain up and givin' 'er a go. A small-town pull is more fun than the big events in cities where the monster tractors show up. At a small-town event, guys with "stock" tractors souped up a bit come out to play. It's good, clean, wholesome fun, something from Andy Griffith.

LET THE MUSIC PLAY

Footfalls echo in the memory
Down the passage which we did not take
Towards the door we never opened

T. S. Eliot

DAY 26 • RHINELAND TO MARTHASVILLE, MISSOURI

A stunning September sunrise warms the morning around me as I stand on the back porch of The Doll House before breakfast the next morning, breathing in the moist midwestern morning air. With only 20 or 30 miles in front of us today, we take our time and enjoy the excellent breakfast Amanda lays out for us, fulfilling nicely the stereotype of wholesome and delicious home cooking.

Out on the trail and headed east at a leisurely pace, our ride rolls along the plain of the river, crossing many bridges, ducking in and out of the woods and under the bluffs. For the last few miles before reaching Marthasville, the trail pulls away from the river, running along at the edge of the forest where the hills come down to kiss the farmland of the floodplain.

The last mile of our day leaves the flat trail and climbs a steep road up to the Concord Hill Bed and Breakfast, run by Maggie and George. It's early in the day, so we explore the town of Marthasville, followed by some quality hot tub time out back before sunset, enjoying a beautiful evening on a great back porch that wraps around a house in a way that only southern architecture knows how to do well.

The comfort I feel around Rick continues to baffle me, making me wonder if we don't create a mental imprint of good friends when we're young, and this imprint renews our friendship immediately when we see each other again 40 years later. I'm sure some level of compatibility has to be there as well, and that there are probably people I knew when I was very young whom I wouldn't get along with now. But there's something fascinating about the connection we seem to hold onto through decades of life. Rick and I enjoy relaxed and comfortable conversation that warms my soul.

Life is full of treasures hiding in plain sight. The life we build around us is a fabric that we weave day to day, and this fabric creates folds and pleats that can hide these treasures. I feel lucky that I've had the time to pull back a fold in life to rediscover my friendship with Rick.

Wandering alone around the old house after a shower, I notice a dark passageway leading down off the living room. It feels just slightly "off limits," but I can't resist the urge to explore. How much harm can come from just peeking around the corner? Then the next corner . . .

There, tucked away down some stairs and around a corner, is a wine cellar, set up like a little speakeasy. Warmed by the notion of finding something secret, I'm excited by the sense of *discovery* that happens when we stumble into a secret place like this. I look forward to sharing this new discovery, maybe playing some cards and partaking in some of the libations available behind the bar.

Wandering back up the stairs into the living room, I notice the edges of the room are filled with musical instruments laying around. I wander over to a beautiful Martin D-35 that seems to be calling my name, and I glance around to see if I can find some reason I shouldn't pick this gorgeous guitar up and play a little bit. I don't look very hard for discouragement before reaching down and tenderly lifting this treasure from its open case. The polished wood of the instrument is warm in my hands, and its voice reaches sweetly into the empty room as I pluck the strings with my right hand, my left hand caressing a couple of chords from the neck.

There's magic in a gem like this. Alchemy born when the craftsman chose the wood and began gluing pieces of it together. The soul of the instrument evolving and maturing as musicians held her in their arms, coaxing sweet sounds, their souls in harmony with that of the instrument. Sweet song blooming from this wood, drawing the soul just a little further along its path of evolution.

I feel this rich soul in my arms as my meager little sounds are added to the beauty the instrument has produced. Feeling a presence beside me, I turn to see a fella sitting on the couch not far away, smiling. Self-conscious, I stumble a bit, feeling very much like I imagine a man might feel who was hugging another man's wife and her husband walked in on them.

"I'm so sorry—is this your guitar?" Pushing the guitar toward him, a sense of guilt is dripping from me.

Smiling, he motions with his hands for me to keep the guitar. "No please—keep playing. She's a beautiful instrument, isn't she?"

"Gorgeous. But honestly, I'm really embarrassed that I just helped myself to your guitar. Thanks for not making me feel bad."

He gives me a broad aw shucks smile with a little half shrug. "Heck, ain't nothin' to regret in the doin' of something. My regrets are all for instruments I should have picked up but didn't."

I think about his words for just a minute. Do I really want to get into a philosophical discussion with this guy, or just thank him for letting me play his guitar then move on? Not one to miss many opportunities to banter ontology, I reply.

"Oh I don't know, I imagine there are quite a few things I've *done* that I *regret doing*."

"Maybe you're right. I know there's a bunch of stuff I wish I'd done differently, or said differently, but not many I feel like I *regret*. I'd just fine-tune the execution next time." Pausing, he looks thoughtfully into the distance through the window. "But real regrets? All those are the *I could'a done but didn't* category. At least all of 'em I can think of." He stands as he speaks and crosses the room to kneel down beside me.

I feel the fingers of my left hand alternating between a C and a G chord, throwing a little minor in there now and then, the fingers of my right hand walking along the strings in a clumsy Travis pattern. Pretty quickly I become aware of the quiet around us as he listens to me play. I've never been able to get past my self-consciousness when it comes to making music. I'm just a clumsy hack when it comes to bringing a guitar to life, embarrassed to let my self-perceived incompetence show.

It's a personality flaw I wish I could fix. In most of life's arenas, I'm perfectly happy to run with folks who are much better at something than I am. But for some reason, when it comes to music, I can't seem to get over my insecurities. Music is one of those deep soul connections we're able to create or participate in, and I would love to feel more secure in myself.

The self-consciousness turns my fingers into clumsy sticks, and I stop, looking up at him. Awkwardly, I begin to put the guitar back in its case.

"You'll regret it," he smiles at me, reaching over to gently close the lid on the case before I can put the old Martin in. I stop, pulling the old instrument back into my lap. He seems to understand my self-consciousness, and a moment of thoughtful silence is ended when he stands abruptly. "Listen, I gotta run into town and pick up George and the rest of my buddies at the bar. We'll be back in an hour or so, and we'll play music together. We'd love it if you join us, but at the very least, keep my guitar company while I'm gone."

He walks out of the room without a backwards glance. I

cradle the old instrument for a few minutes more, softly picking through a few minor chords, then set it gently back in its case. Glancing back over my shoulder as I make my way out of the living room, the beautiful old Martin looks back at me, wondering why I'm leaving it alone. I almost go back and pick her up again, cursing the lack of courage that keeps me moving out of the room.

An hour or so later, as we emerge from playing cards and drinking beer down in the speakeasy, I notice the old Martin still beckoning to me from the edge of the room, where she lies quietly with the other instruments, waiting for George and the crew to come home from the bar. I wander over and gaze down at her. Alone in the room, I gently draw her onto my lap, my clumsy fingers coaxing soft sounds that fill my heart and soul with gladness. It seems like only a short while until self-doubt creeps around the corner and steals the bliss that the Martin and I are sharing. I know I should keep playing, should keep falling into the moment of joy I've discovered, but the real musicians might walk through the door at any moment, and what if they see me or hear me?

Truly, we only regret the things we fail to do.

The opportunities we fail to grasp.

The things we fail to say.

The instruments we fail to play . . .

It's late in the night when the music gets underway down in the living room. The cool September night air feels good creeping in through my open window, the quiet disturbed only by wonderful sounds from the living room below, filling the air with the songs of musicians expressing themselves through the souls of their instruments. Their music drifts out through the windows downstairs, across the old porch, and folds itself luxuriantly around me in my bed above.

Music has been an unexpected and delightful surprise to me as I've crossed Missouri. A little further up the trail we talked to a fella named Doug who runs the Rendleman Home B&B, who shared with us how much their place revolves around the music that gets played there every night. Tonight George and his friends weave together a delicious blend of seventies folk music, rock & roll, and deep bluegrass to serenade me as I lie in bed, feeling a couple of competing emotions.

On the one hand, I'm appreciating at a very deep level my rediscovered friendship with Rick. On the other hand, I ruminate over the regrets that seem to seep out of deep wells in my life now and then, wondering why I let myself drop more down into those wells when they already feel like they're at capacity. Too many things unsaid, too many deeds undone . . .

A peculiar cocktail of emotions, but I suppose some of life's greatest epiphanies come from these sorts of odd mixes. We stumble through life, knowing where we are and where we're going, pretty sure of our path, when we turn a corner and decide to explore a stairway, discovering something that lights up our day in a way we didn't expect. Then we turn another corner, and confront an insecurity to wrestle with, a failure to own.

A new path, a new route, a new room, a new way of seeing something, a new way to experience life. New music to hear.

Maybe it's just a matter of what we're ready for at the time. Our *place in life* probably has a lot to do with what the universe decides to drop in front of us. A whole lot of what the universe drops in front of us was probably there all along, but we weren't ready to see it yet. Some combination of what we're ready for in life, what we need in life, what lessons we need to learn from life, or what someone else needs from us.

An open heart, a curious mind, and a willing soul. Keeping our eyes tuned for those small passageways that might lead us to a place we need to go, keeping our ears open for some music off in the distance we might need to hear. Being open enough to see a beautiful old Martin sitting in the corner when we cross paths with one another.

When the universe drops something like that in front of us, we need to pick it up and play!

BREAKFAST WITH GEORGE

Love one another, but make not a bond of love: Let it rather be a moving sea between the shores of your souls.
Kahlil Gibran

DAY 27 • MARTHASVILLE, MISSOURI TO ALTON, ILLINOIS

I'm up and rattling around the house early the next morning, hoping to find some food. I'll part paths with Rick today, riding on to the end of the trail and beyond while he returns home, and we're hoping to have breakfast early.

Early breakfast isn't gonna happen. Clearly, the merry-making of last night has resulted in slow and measured movement this morning, and Maggie makes it clear to us that once George hits the kitchen to start breakfast, everybody needs to stay out of the way. Our hoped-for 8:00 breakfast is clearly on a delay, and "forks up" isn't likely to happen for quite some time.

A note of moderate importance. I'm a breakfast guy. I need breakfast. I really enjoy breakfast. Lunch is nice, but it's just sustenance. Supper I can take or leave, and generally sleep better without it anyway. But breakfast? That's not a meal I'm good at skipping or delaying. For me, 8:00 is pretty late for breakfast as it is, and this undetermined time for a delayed breakfast has me feeling uneasy.

So I pace a bit, watching as George ambles into the kitchen. He's focused on the coffee pot, emitting a distinct *don't bother me* vibe.

George doesn't appear to be happy with the morning, wincing at any loud noise that invades his space. He's a creature of late-night fun, who clearly struggles to find much good about the early morning. Yet, here we are, guests of his *bed and breakfast,* done with *bed* and waiting for the *breakfast.* With great deliberation, he begins his work.

George strikes me as a man seeking deep Zen harmony as he begins to orchestrate the components of what will become our breakfast. Ingredients from the garden and the refrigerator come together on the countertops like tributaries flowing toward a rich river. Magic is in the air around the kitchen at Concord Hill, which only stokes my hunger.

I pace, grabbing some fruit when I can. George is like a bear guarding his den as he moves around his sanctuary, clearly not happy that I'm encroaching, scavenging scraps while he tries to cook. George has the advantage of sharp kitchen utensils within easy reach, but I have the advantage of a well-rested body with quick reflexes. There are a couple of close calls accompanied by growls and grunts, the bear chasing the scavenger off his territory, the scavenger reaching in for a quick bite now and then.

Maggie finally convinces me to go outside to enjoy the beautiful autumn morning while we patiently anticipate breakfast, assuring me that it will be worth the wait. Humph. Patience my ass. It's past breakfast time, and I'm hungry.

The tension evaporates around 10:00 as we sit down to what can only be described as an orgy of breakfast delight. My gushing praise of the food (when people can understand my garbled speech around mouthfuls of heaven) seems to ease George's bad temper, and we eventually find peace in relative proportion to my consumption of breakfast and George's consumption of strong coffee.

A couple of hours later, 10 or 15 miles further up the trail at Augusta, I'm saying my good-byes. Rick will turn around here and head back to Concord Hill to pack up his car and start for home. Mounting up and heading east by myself, I glance into the mirror on my helmet, watching the receding image of someone who I've known nearly all my life. The past days have been joy-full to me, enjoying friendship that's aged and grown for a lifetime. We dawdled a lot, riding at an easy pace, taking the time to explore, chat, discover . . .

Deep and powerful emotions accompany lifelong friendships, and the value of old friends is greater than I usually let myself recognize. I admire people who are good at maintaining those friendships, feeding them and nurturing them. I realize that I'm not, and that I'm poorer for it. I'm grateful for these last couple of days of casual riding along the trail, discovering new layers of friendship.

As the figure in the mirror grows smaller, I feel something wet on my cheeks, and I'm pretty sure it isn't the wind that's pulling tears from my eyes. Behind me I feel the comfort of friendship that's old in my lifetime, and I recognize the poverty in my failure to accept that comfort gracefully and well.

Ahead of me, the adventure of the unknown whispers to me in the breeze caressing my face. A restless spirit pushes my legs as they begin to pour coal to the pedals, racing ahead down the path, chasing a future I know nothing of, other than the soft voice of what might have been, or might be . . .

Letting my legs run loose, I race east on the trail, kicking the pace up to a high level and keeping it there for hours. Am I chasing, I wonder, or being chased? By what? For what?

The closer I get to St. Louis, the more crowded the trail is with folks out enjoying a beautiful autumn day along this treasure of a pathway. I nearly fly past a Ted Drewes that's right along the trail. I rein myself in, turn around, and wheel into the little shop. (Ted Drewes is a local St. Louis chain that serves up the best frozen custard on earth—at least that's the story that everyone in the St. Louis area sticks to. And really, it is good.)

Sitting outside with my frozen custard, watching the people, I wonder why there aren't more destinations like this along bike trails. Out here in the middle of nowhere, Ted Drewes was smart enough to open a little shop, and they're doing a land office business. I chat briefly with a couple who started riding this morning at a trailhead 10 miles up the trail, are enjoying their custard here, then will ride back to their car. I imagine a lot of the folks here this morning are doing the same thing.

We want to ride *to something*, for a *reason*. Sure we could drive down to the Ted Drewes that's a mile from our house, but this is better. It's a bike ride to Ted Drewes. It's a point *B*, and we usually need a point B—a place to be going to.

Reflecting back on the ride across the Katy Trail, I realize that the trail is beautiful, feels remote, and is a pleasure to ride on. But there just aren't very many point *B*s along the trail. I wonder how much more use the trail would get if there were.

It's one of those oddities of human behavior. We need a place to go to. We're not very good at things like wandering down the trail to enjoy a beautiful autumn morning; we need a reason to go somewhere and a place to be going to.

Hey, I get it—*I'm* not just wandering down the trail. I'm headed to a point *B*. It's just that my point *B* is still 1000 miles away.

Looking around at the folks milling around together, sharing their custard, I'm reminded of another of those little human oddities: our need for crowds. Humans generally like to crowd into the middle where everyone else is. We're afraid of the edges, out where there aren't many people. I remember how surprised I was long ago when I came to understand the marketing principles that guide how restaurants decide where to set up, and why shopping areas are generally clustered together.

The mall.

We like to say it's about convenience, and that it just makes logical sense to have things together so it's easier to shop. But I don't think that's all of it. I think it's about us feeling comfortable when we all march together into the middle where everyone else is. The comfort of the crowd milling around us. Not unlike the wildebeest crowding together, avoiding the edges where the predators have easier access. It's not everybody, but it's enough of a majority that our civilization is designed for the wildebeest in our culture.

Finishing my custard, I mount up and head east down the trail. By myself. Fleeing the middle. Headed toward my point B. Alone.

Life is good.

By early afternoon I'm kicking around the old river town of St. Charles, enjoying a sandwich at a little café just off the trail. It seems that St. Charles is a common place for folks in the St. Louis area to drive to, unload the bikes, and take a little ride on the trail. Maybe all the way to Ted Drewes . . . While St. Charles isn't the end of the trail, it's the last *destination* along the trail.

I talk to several cyclists, looking for anyone who can give me advice about what happens when the trail actually ends about 10 or 15 miles further northeast, and whether the roads across the bridge into Alton, Illinois are safe for a cyclist. Most of the people I talk to aren't aware that the trail even goes northeast from here, and of those few who are aware, none have ever ridden that way.

There's no point B, and it's *way* too far from the middle. I rest my case.

THE MISSISSIPPI AND BEYOND

The blunting effects of slavery upon the slaveholder's moral perceptions are known and conceded the world over; and a privileged class, an aristocracy, is but a band of slaveholders under another name.

Mark Twain, *A Connecticut Yankee in King Arthur's Court*

Greenville, Il

St. Charles, Mo

THE BUTLER'S QUARTERS

I slept and I dreamed that life is all joy. I woke and I saw that life is all service. I served and I saw that service is joy.

Kahlil Gibran

From St. Charles it's about 12 miles to the *actual* end of the trail in Machens. The trail meanders through beautiful farmland along the wide floodplain where the Missouri River finds the Mississippi River. Winding my way along rural roads after the trail ends, I find the feel of pavement beneath my tires comforting after the last couple of hundred miles of crusher fines along the Katy.

West Alton is a tiny little place, and the last town in Missouri on my route. There's a country fair of some sort going on, and the place is packed with old tractors, presumably there for a tractor pull later in the day. I stop and admire some of the old machines before continuing east across the Mississippi River into Alton, Illinois.

An old riverboat town, Alton was a prosperous place back in its 19th-century heyday, complete with an elite class of barons who lived up on the hill overlooking town. Depending on your point of view, these folks might have been robber barons or titans of enterprise. Either way, they had most of the wealth, and had the big houses up on the hill.

I find my way to the Beall Mansion up on that hill. The Beall Mansion is a beautifully restored place, and after Jim checks me in and we lock my bike in the garage, he shows me the back stairway up which I schlep my stuff to the top floor. The Beall Mansion isn't a cheap accommodation, and the only room I'm willing to pay for is the Butler's Quarters. (Note that when I checked in the innkeeper referred to this as the Butler's Quarters, but generally they refer to it as the Servants' Quarters.

Back in the olden days, when a more obvious class system in America was alive and well, rich folks needed a way for the servants to maneuver through the house without being seen. Rich folks didn't want too much exposure to poor folks, and things like back stairways served the dual purpose of reducing traffic and wear and tear on the nice stuff and keeping the servants out of sight of the people of power and influence performing deeds of power and influence.

In the era when this home was built, much of the world still embraced the notion of an *aristocracy,* a class of people who *deserved* to rule and control. Trundling up the sturdy staircase, I wonder if we've moved very far from that framework of aristocracy, even as we convince ourselves that there's great freedom and equality in our culture. Is this seeking of a hierarchy just a part of our makeup as humans?

This old stairway is rough and well-made, capable of handling a lot of traffic. If history is any indicator, the back stairway is where most of the traffic will continue to flow.

Arriving finally at the top floor, I find the perfect place for me at this exact time along this ride. The Butler's Quarters is snug and cozy, but in a relatively manly way. Hard to describe, but clearly, this is a good place for me. The sound of birds singing high in the trees outside floats through the open windows. This place feels good.

By the time I get showered, wash my clothes in the sink and hang them to dry, it's too late to find supper anywhere close. So I wander down to the main floor, where there's a lasciviously large assortment of chocolates and candies of all sorts. There's a little "almost healthy" food too, but mostly I just devour chocolate in a quite conspicuous and opulent fashion.

In the corner of one room I discover a decanter of brandy, from which I pour liberally into a snifter that sits invitingly nearby. Good brandy is the perfect partner for an orgy of chocolate, a relationship that I cultivate fervently while sitting in the stately Victorian room by myself.

Is it any wonder that the obscenely wealthy find it so easy to justify their decadence? I find it an easy thing to understand as I enjoy the rich opulence of the room, the mansion, the brandy, the chocolate. I'm happy, relaxed, comfortable, and satisfied. Pleased.

And at the same time, a bit self conscious of the symbol of excess that I'm enjoying, maybe even slightly ashamed of myself. How easy it is for us to traverse the lines, outraged one minute at some depravity, easily ignoring that decadence the next minute when we feel some benefit or comfort from it.

It's good to be king.

Is this a common sentiment—this tinge of offense and shame in the midst of excess? Similar, maybe, to the sense of guilt that survivors of a tragedy sometimes feel, their unconscious minds not able to reconcile their survival with the misfortune of those whom they were with. Does luxury suck us down into a self-loathing that we try to soothe with more effusive wealth? Could that be part of the addiction to power and wealth—the belief that with enough of it, we'll stop feeling regret over the good we fail to do with the gifts we're given?

Loaded up on a chocolate high, mellowed by some delicious brandy, I drift toward sleep in my butler's room. Alone in my little corner of the universe tonight, I'm happy and content. This tiny room high in this old mansion feels like a good place for me. We've all got our place, or maybe a set of places that work well for us. Don't get me wrong—I don't like it one bit when a few people *lord their power* over other people, and *keep them in their place.* I'm a stubborn SOB who'll argue with a rock if I think the rock is trying to tell me what to do.

But we've all got places that *feel right* to us, and we all need to decide and figure out for ourselves what and where *our place* is. It probably changes as we move through life, as life happens around us, and we mold ourselves into our ever-changing self with life's help.

I do believe I have a place, or maybe a set of places, that suit me well. I like being in a *place* where I can provide service, where I can help other folks in some way. I see this reflected in many aspects of my life. In my career now, I like positions where I can sit in the background and be a quiet advisor and mentor to folks—usually younger than me and full of ambition—to help them do their jobs and advance their careers. I'm done with big corner offices; I prefer the quiet place to sit, observe, listen, and be of service and value when I can.

I like the Butler's Quarters. It suits me well. It's a good place for me at this point in my life.

A DOSE OF DISCOMFORT

*A little misery sweetens existence. It is the salt
that makes it palatable and wholesome.*

Eliza Cook, *Diamond Dust*

DAY 28 • ALTON TO GREENVILLE, ILLINOIS

It's well before dawn as I amble down the servant's stairwell after an excellent night's sleep in the Butler's Quarters. The silent opulence of the main floor stands in stark contrast to the simple utility of the hidden passages built for servants. The house feels quiet and solid this morning. In the 19th century, it would have been only the servants up and about at this hour, quietly preparing the house for the "master."

In their place. Being of service. Which is what most of the great gurus, shaman, and religious leaders throughout history have preached. With rare exceptions, those great leaders have pressed their followers to seek the *path of service.*

The predawn quiet of this old mansion sheds clarity on this *upside-down-ness* of how we build our *classes* as humans. Those folks who delude themselves into thinking they're on top of the structure because they hold power and money may just be the ones furthest from realizing their real human and spiritual potential. (Easier for a camel to pass through the eye of a needle, or something like that, as I recall . . .)

I gobble a bit of the endless chocolate spread throughout this opulent old mansion, enjoying the last few minutes of my little journey into the ostentatious world of 19th-century aristocracy. I wander into the kitchen pantry and find a bit of actual nutrition. I bid good-bye to Jim as I collect my bike from the garage, then pedal down the driveway into the dim predawn light.

The streets are empty at this favorite hour of mine before everyone wakes. Damp air heavy around me feels brisk in the quiet, early morning chill. My bike quietly coasts along the mansion-lined streets at the top of the hill above Alton. After a few blocks, the street drops sharply into the historic old river town, past the casino riverboat that's quiet at this hour, and finally onto a nice paved bicycle path that follows the top of the levy along the mighty Mississippi.

After five or six miles I drop off the levy path and onto roads that meander through an industrial area full of what appear to be refineries for a few miles. Luckily it's early, so I'm able to sneak my bike through this area that I imagine is anything *but* bike friendly when there's more activity.

My Garmin finds the Madison County Transit Watershed Trail, which I follow for a few miles into Edwardsville. I find breakfast at a diner named Fiona's on Main, savoring a little dry time out of the light rain. I wander around town, finding a bike store where I pick up a couple of extra tire tubes to replace a couple I've used to fix flats, then follow my Garmin to the Madison County Nickel Plate Trail.

Twenty miles later, the trail drops me onto Highway 140 at Alhambra, where I appreciate a few minutes of refuge in a convenience store. The wet and heavy air from earlier this morning morphed into a light mist a couple of hours ago, and has further devolved into a steady light rain. I have 20 miles to

ride in the rain on this highway before my day ends in Greenville, and I dilly-dally in the store a good bit, hoping for some
clearing, but all that's clear is that this rain is getting heavier.

Riding a bicycle on the highway in the rain is miserable.
I'm pretty sure that if I looked up the word "miserable" in
Wikipedia, it would say something like this:

> (of a situation or environment) causing someone to
> feel wretchedly unhappy or uncomfortable. "The
> miserable gray sky dripped cold water all along the
> highway, soaking the cyclist as he pedaled hard to
> try to stay warm. Each passing car or truck drenched
> him with grimy mist, sometimes dumping large
> quantities of splashed water from their tires when
> they passed too closely."

> SYNONYMS: tragic, gloomy, pathetic, sad, wretched,
> dreary, dismal, drab, depressing, grim, cheerless, bleak,
> desolate, poor, shabby, squalid, seedy, dilapidated, un-
> pleasant, disagreeable, depressing, wet, rainy, stormy

> ANTONYMS: luxurious, glorious, lovely, dry, wonderful,
> warm

This sucks. The world closes in around me. My focus
sharpens and narrows. Every ounce of me goes into staying
warm and safe. While part of me would like to stop, the hard
pedaling keeps the furnace burning inside me, warming me
inside my soaked clothes. There's world around me on both
sides, but all I can see is the pavement right in front of me. I
don't want my wheels on the white line because it's so slick in
the rain, and I need to watch out for wheel-eating holes in the
pavement that could be hidden by puddles.

A wet highway is a very lonely place on a bicycle.

These are midwesterners passing me in the cars, which
means they're just a little nicer than folks in other regions of

the country might be. They might be feeling sorry for the soaking wet guy shivering on the bike as they pass, or they might be giving me room because they wonder what kind of idiot doesn't know any better than to get in out of the rain.

In either case, they seem to give me just a little more space as they pass, and for this I'm grateful.

Waddling into a diner once I reach Greenville, water squishing from me with every step, I notice that folks give me a wide berth as I pass. I can only imagine what a lugubrious sight I must be. (A tip of the hat to Carl Hiaasen about here . . .) One hot burger later, I'm feeling much more human and loved, despite the continued excommunication I feel from the other patrons in the diner.

Walking out of the diner, I look up into a sky that has brightened slightly, having apparently decided it's dropped enough water for the day. I mount up and make my way to the B&B where I'll stay tonight, where Nancy (the innkeeper) happens to be standing at the door to welcome me. My mood has brightened in direct (and inverse) proportion to the moisture falling from the sky, and Nancy's southern hospitality warms my spirit even further.

A hot shower completes my transformation back into a cheerful human being, and I make my way downstairs to visit with Nancy a bit. She's a southern lady through and through, who clearly loves the chance to share her southern roots and hospitality with guests at her inn. My spirit warms further as I listen to her story, sipping tea, snacking on a dish of something sweet she's set on the table for me.

Lying comfortably in bed later in the evening, I realize that my mind is building memories already of Nancy's warm hospitality and kind spirit. Oh sure, the cold and wet still lingers there on the edge of my memory as well, but it's the warmth that's making its way to the front of my memory. The healing and delighting properties of food, human companionship, and a warm and dry place never cease to amaze me.

We live comfortable lives. Discomfort isn't part of the everyday existence of most Americans. We turn the faucet, and hot water comes out whenever we want it. Cold? Just turn up the thermostat a little bit. When's the last time most of us were soaked to the bone and shivering violently from the cold? When's the last time most of us were deeply frightened that the cars and trucks passing us in the rain on the highway wouldn't be able to see us? When's the last time most of us felt deeply alone and isolated in the world, thankful for the smallest gestures of courtesy from those passing us?

I'm not advocating that cold or danger or fear are good for us, or that we should seek them out. But when we build a life of such comfort that we forget what deep cold feels like, or forget what mortal fear does to our mind, or forget just how delicious a kindness can taste . . . Well, is that good?

Does the absence of discomfort keep us from true appreciation of comfort? When we never feel the darkness around us, does brilliance fade into the mundane? When we forget that we can survive misery, do we make ourselves prey to the attraction of mediocrity?

A WINTER NIGHT IN THE DARK WOODS

The lust for comfort murders the passions of the soul.
Khalil Gibran

Many years ago (decades really), my brother Erik and I drove a tractor-trailer together. You know the kind—the big semi's you see out on the highway. This was back in the seventies.

There's a good bit of fun backstory that leads up to the story I'm about to tell, and the story generally gets better in the telling when it's told over a couple of beers. The important part of the backstory is that I had accepted orders for a pickup we needed to make, and the orders took us further into the mountains than we had any business taking the big truck.

I'll pick the story up at a place deep in the Arkansas mountains, on a narrow and steep old logging road. A winter storm was rolling in on us, and the fuel filter on the truck had gelled up, shutting the truck down on a steep uphill grade along the logging road in the middle of the woods as the winter night closed around us.

"So what now, Mr. Hotshot?" Erik's tone has roots well beyond that current mechanical problem. His anger about our situation reached back to the beginning of the day, when he had warned me that it was a bad idea to try to get our big semi back into the mountains to make the pickup in the first place. I had dismissed his fears with an assurance that we'd be able to maneuver the roads, and of course I had made the matter worse with continued dismissals throughout the morning as we threaded our way deeper onto steep mountain roads that got narrower, twistier, and steeper with each passing mile.

We'd spent the day loading our truck as it was parked on the gravel road, blocking passage from either direction. Not that anyone had been trying to get by; I'm pretty sure the middle of nowhere was visible from where we were. A couple of hours before we had finished, a dense winter fog had rolled in on top of us, with temperatures hovering right around freezing. By the time we were ready to go, backing the big rig down the road we'd come up (this was our exit strategy) was no longer an option, because the thick fog obscured the back of my trailer through my mirrors.

So we went forward, on a road that would take us deeper into the mountains, but would eventually deliver us to the sort of paved highway that this truck was designed to be on. It's actually a bit of a stretch to call the gravel beneath our tires a *road*—it was really something between a logging road and a jeep trail.

A little more about Neil and Erik: we love each other dearly, but I can drive the poor man crazy sometimes. Erik's a safe and thoughtful man. If he's gonna buy a new boat, he'll think about it for months, shop for more months, and ponder and analyze for more months yet, before finally arriving at the decision. Then he'll shop some more before making the purchase. Conversely, I'll learn enough to decide which boat I want, then I'll be hooking it up to the truck and on the way to the lake tomorrow.

We complement each other quite nicely, one of us keeping us alive, the other pushing us headlong into some adventure or another. You can guess which is which. Once, while skiing in Colorado, Erik and I came to some yellow boundary ropes—the ones that tell skiers that they're not supposed to cross, because the terrain on the other side is too steep, or the avalanche danger is too high, or any number of reasons why the terrain is dangerous and off-limits.

"So what do the yellow ropes mean?" Erik asked.

"Just that it's steep back on that side, and that there are lots of trees," I told him, as I lifted the rope for him to go under.

"You sure about this?"

"We'll be fine." This dismissive tone must be *soooo* annoying.

Ten minutes later, we were tangled in a quagmire of dense trees and deep powder on a very steep slope. Erik looked at me and exclaimed, "That's it! I'm done. I'm walking out of here before I kill myself on these skis."

Well, if you've skied, you know that this isn't really an option in snow that's deep and soft. Colorado's beautiful light champagne powder is heaven to ski on top of, but take one step off your skies and your legs will post-hole down to your hips in the stuff, though you'll still be suspended far above any actual terra firma. I tried to be helpful and share this useful information with Erik, but he had zero tolerance for any more of the nonsense that his brother was spewing at that particular moment.

Fifteen seconds later, he was looking up at me with fury in his eyes, having immediately sunk to his hips into the six or eight feet of glorious light Colorado white heaven that our skis had been floating on. I'm pretty sure I learned some new curse words that day, or at least new ways to combine curse words in creative and interesting ways I hadn't heard before.

Ten minutes more passed before Erik had his skis on and we continued down the mountain. I kept a safe distance from him to let him cool off a bit, since I was pretty sure somebody would get hurt if he could get his hands on me. I don't think I've ever heard anybody keep an angry rant going for as long as he did that day. We eventually made it down the mountain safely. Nobody got injured, mostly because he'd cooled off by the time we reached the bottom and decided not to do bodily harm to his reckless brother.

That's us, Erik and me. He's weighing the options, wanting to make sure the decision is right, and I'm crashing headlong into the risk, confident we'll figure it out as we go. A nice balance of cautious deliberation and reckless zeal. So far, nobody's gotten seriously hurt.

I'm pretty sure he'll outlive me.

Back in Arkansas, on the cold mountain in the dense fog and freezing rain, Erik was not a happy man.

"So now what, Mr. Brilliant?" He wasn't so much talking to me or asking me a question as throwing the words at me. "You just HAD to drive up this God-forsaken mountain, didn't you? We could have been safely down the highway by now! We could have just told the dispatcher the truck couldn't make this pickup. But no, Mr. Hotshot thinks he can do it! Well, wadyathink now, Mr. Hotshot? Now that we're stuck out here where IF WE'RE LUCKY we'll freeze to death before the boys from *Deliverance* land come for a play date!"

We were on a steep slope, but the brakes seemed to be holding just fine once I'd set them. I'd crawled out of the cab and thrown chocks behind a couple of wheels as he was ranting at me. He'd have been less mad at me if I'd seemed bothered by our situation, but I was just standing in front of the truck, shrugging my shoulders. "So, you staying here with the truck, or coming with me?"

"Coming with you? WHERE?! We skipped breakfast and haven't eaten anything all day. I'm cold and hungry, and you don't have a plan, do you?"

"Well, I'm not sure yet," I answered, "but we gotta do something, and it'll involve getting somewhere besides here. All I know right now is that we gotta get someplace to find a winch or a fuel filter or something. We can't just sit here and freeze."

Logic. He hates it when I do that.

He was right, of course. The smart thing to have done would have been to listen to him way back at the beginning of the day. It was my stupidity that had put us into that mess. In my mind, the door on that barn had been swinging open for a long time, and there was no sense in revisiting it. Yep, I had been an idiot, but we were where we were, so we needed to move forward.

Really though, he had probably needed to hear me say the words. "You're right." I'm sure I didn't say them. I doubt if I ever do.

So, for the record, here it is: *"Erik, you were right that day, and I should have listened to you. Sorry about that."*

The woods we were traipsing through probably weren't all that populated with humans at any time, and on that cold winter night in the freezing rain, our odds of finding a living human had probably been hovering below the temperature reading. There wasn't a house anywhere. In the back of my mind, a faint banjo riff from *Deliverance* was starting to ring in my ears.

After a couple of miles we came to an old shack. There was just a dim light shining through the window, but we were hoping someone was home. Maybe they had a winch and chains, or maybe we could use their phone to call somebody who might have such equipment, or something.

Knocking on the door, we stepped back a bit to make sure we weren't too threatening when someone opened the door. I suspect we were a sorry sight.

The door slowly opened, coming to a rest halfway, and the first thing we saw was the barrel of a side-by-side leveled at us. Behind the shotgun an old guy peered at us, wondering what we wanted. The big picture descended on me at that moment, and I realized we might have been the first visitors at that guy's door in a very long time, and here we came in the middle of a winter storm. His clothes were ragged, and he had seen some hard miles in life. He may not have had indoor plumbing, or running water. He may not have had electricity. Heck, he didn't even have teeth. (Well, in fairness, he seemed to have a few. "Summer teeth," as my friend Tony calls them—some 'er teeth, some aren't.)

The old guy wasn't about to trust us, and the shotgun

stayed leveled at us. He told us that if we kept going down that road, we'd come to his daughter's house in about five miles or so. We'd know we were close when we saw the big oak tree on the left, and we should look for the path of her driveway on the right just past that.

Really? An oak tree? We were in a bloody forest of big oak trees!

But I wasn't gonna argue with him. Well, I might have been willing to argue with *him,* but I wasn't going to argue with the side-by-side he had pointed at my chest.

I have wonderful memories of our cold walk in the dark wet forest that night. It really was beautiful. The soft rain had a "tinkle" sound to it as it hit dried leaves and branches, and it had mostly frozen by the time it landed. As we walked, the trees creaked and snapped occasionally, shifting under the weight of ice building on their branches. The snow fell intermittently, softening the sound of the world around us, muting the quiet crunch of our boots on the path. Everything was covered in a sparkling hoar frost from the fog.

That sort of walk brings a new focus to life. We were alone. Really alone in the quiet woods. I suppose we could have frozen to death, but I knew that wouldn't happen. We would keep walking, and we would solve this. But it *could* have happened, and that realization brought a different focus.

It was cold. Really cold. A bone-soaked cold. A dark and lonely cold.

The first glimpse of that next house five miles later brought a flood of warm emotion to both of us. The gal welcomed us with open arms. There was hot chili on the kitchen stove, the best food I ever put in my mouth, made so by the 24 hours or so that had passed since I last ate. Our clothes ended up strung around the family room to dry in the heat of the wood stove, while we huddled in borrowed bathrobes, sucking down the chili, letting the heat soak in.

It's one of my most pleasant memories in life, that little cabin in the Arkansas mountains. I think the woman's name was Sheri, but I'm not positive. She was truly an angel for Erik and me that night. Her warm chili, piping-hot stove, and pleasant company was such a contrast to our cold night that it remains burned in my memory, resting in that bucket of wonderful experiences.

Without the cold misery that led up to meeting Sheri, would I have held on to the memory of that cabin in the woods?

I don't want to seek out misery on my path. But I do want to seek life—all of life. In doing so, I accept that I'll sometimes dig myself into some misery. It's only through the lens of misery that some miracles are visible.

Only through loneliness that some levels of deep kindness and compassion can be recognized.

Only through shivering cold that the real warmth of a hearth can be appreciated.

Only through real and empty hunger that a bowl of chili can be truly enjoyed.

Laying in my warm room in Greenville, Illinois, thinking back on my day as I drift toward sleep, I realize that while I didn't enjoy the cold today, I'm thankful to have survived the misery of the rain and the danger on the highway. Nancy's hospitality, company, and nourishment here in her home was heavenly after such a day. My discomfort earlier in the day helped me feel the comfort and magical goodness in the world this afternoon. The light this evening is bright and wonderful, far from mundane.

There's nothing on earth,
like a bowl of hot chili,
sitting on a wood stove,
in a warm house,
in the woods,
on a night filled with cold and wet snow.

THE MIDWEST —
IN THE EAST

In our day we don't allow a hundred and thirty years to elapse between glimpses of a marvel. If somebody should discover a creek in the county next to the one that the North Pole is in, Europe and America would start fifteen costly expeditions thither; one to explore the creek, and the other fourteen to hunt for each other.

Mark Twain, *Life on the Mississippi*

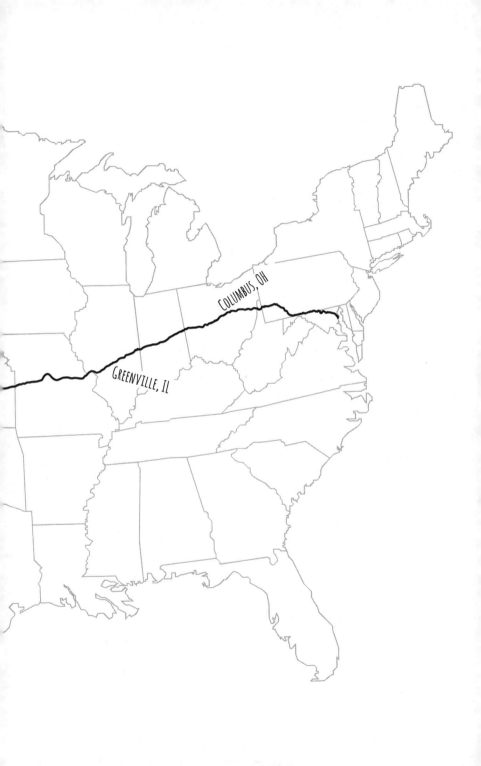

THE OLD NATIONAL ROAD

Two roads diverged in a yellow wood,
And sorry I could not travel both
And be one traveler, long I stood
And looked down one as far as I could
To where it bent in the undergrowth;

. . .

I shall be telling this with a sigh
Somewhere ages and ages hence:
Two roads diverged in a wood, and I—
I took the one less traveled by,
And that has made all the difference.

Robert Frost, "The Road Not Taken"

DAY 29 • GREENVILLE, ILLINOIS TO TERRA HAUTE, INDIANA

Roads are the lifeblood of a civilization.

One of those clichés, I know, but a truer cliché never existed.

It's not *just* about an economy and the need to move goods and services back and forth. It's not *just* about extended family, and the love, acceptance, and cultural sharing that can only occur when folks can go back and forth between camps or tribes. It's the basis of everything that creates a civilization. Without a way to move back and forth, groups of people are individual tribes. Let them move easily from one camp to another, and the tribes can meld together into a civilization.

Roads make the concept of *nation* possible. The Roman Empire became a thing in large part because they had engineers who could build amazing roads that were practical and durable. Heck, in my life I've been on roads that the Romans built that are still usable and durable, millennia later!

There were roads in North America long before Europeans invaded. There were nations and civilizations in North America for hundreds of generations before a bunch of folks on the east coast declared certain truths to be self-evident. The nations that existed here were connected and nurtured by a great network of roads that meandered from one coast to the other, evolving as time went by and the shape of the nations transformed.

Highway 40 holds the unique honor of being the first American highway. Back in 1802 a "National Road" was commissioned by our young nation, and over time this National Road evolved, as did our naming conventions for roads and highways. The National Road used the route of the Cumberland Pike as its foundation, and continued to expand west, finding its way all the way to the Mississippi River before our lexicon changed, and our network of roads and highways was beginning to take on numbers rather than names.

The National Road became US Highway 40, though for years people still called it the National Road. As our cultural lingo evolved, and we all grew accustomed to referring to our highways with numbers, cultural memory created the term *Old National Road* to refer to US 40. Even as it was improved and extended to accommodate the rapidly evolving automobile, folks still referred to it as the Old National Road.

Our insatiable demand for better roads drove us to flatten them and straighten them to accommodate increasing vehicle speeds. We widened them to accommodate more vehicles. As we straightened and leveled the old roads, we often needed to change their paths slightly—move them higher up the hill or further from the creek, blast the roadbed through the hill rather than going around it. As the road moved a few hundred yards one way or the other, its moniker moved with it, and the old highway became a more local road and took on a colloquial name again.

With each generation of highway improvement, the US 40 moniker moved from the old road to the new one. Today, if you drive across the Interstate Highway System from D.C. to Salt Lake City, you'll notice that while you'll generally be driving on I-70, most of the time the signs also let you know that you're driving on US 40. And if you look off to your right or left, you'll often see a nice old road running parallel that looks like it might have been a highway at one point.

It probably was. It's probably *Old 40.* Sometimes it might just be a frontage road, sometimes in might have some colloquial name, and sometimes it might have some state or county number, such as Highway 140.

If you get off the interstate highway and drive along that Old 40, you'll occasionally see another road that parallels Old 40. Often, that old road was the first or second generation of the old highway. *Old Old 40,* if you will. The Old National Road that evolved from the Old Cumberland Road.

I told all that story just so I could tell this one: From here in the middle of Illinois to my destination in Annapolis, I'll be roughly following the route of the Old National Road. Often, I'll be riding on some road named Highway 140, and occasionally I'll be on the newest version of US 40. Sometimes I'll be off on a nameless road that was clearly part of the Old National Road, but few people recognize that anymore.

About 10 miles or so into my morning, I pass through Vandalia, which was the western terminus of the original Cumberland Road, or National Road. I'm riding on one of the many sections of the old highway that goes by the moniker *Highway 140.*

Riding along in a chilly 39 degrees, it feels like autumn around me. Leaves are beginning to show some color on the branches that hang over the road, highlighting the lack of truck traffic to beat back the branches overhead. A bright sunrise bathes the roadway in front of me in warm color.

Stopping to chew on a granola bar and drink some water, I look more closely into the woods around me, and notice a tiny old bridge that crosses a little creek. The bridge is swallowed up in the undergrowth extending from the forest behind, making it difficult to see. The creek is small enough that you don't really notice if from the highway, since there's now a culvert buried beneath the highway to carry the water. But more than a century ago, when we were building the National Road, a little bridge is what we took to get across this little creek. That little bridge still stands, over at the edge of the woods, with the clear signs of a flat roadbed leading to it from both directions.

Old Old 40.

I stop and enjoy lunch at Joe Sippers Cafe in Effingham just as the wind starts to pick up. It pushes an empty stroller out into the street, a young mom grabbing it and securing it around the corner out of the wind. A southeast wind. Into my face. Delightful.

I got a later start this morning than I usually do, relaxing over breakfast and a morning chat with Nancy back in Greenville. It's noon, and I'm only halfway through a day that I think is going to be 100 miles long. Spoiler alert: I'm wrong. Today is 121 miles long, so I'm not even halfway. A disheartening moment lurks about 50 or 60 miles further down the road, after I've been beat up by a headwind for much of the day. It's about then that I'll discover I have 15 more miles to ride before arriving at my hot shower and soft bed.

Riding along US 40, I notice that it's quite common for roads with the name *Cumberland* to cut off the highway. These are remnants of the old route of the Cumberland Road, routes that got replaced by the one that I'm riding on. Routes that became replaced by the new version of US 40, which was later replaced by yet newer versions.

In Greenup, Cumberland Road veers away from US 40 as I approach the little town. I veer with the Cumberland Road here, following the old narrow pavement to the place where it crosses the Embarras River on an old covered bridge. This is the first of several covered bridges I'll visit. Each will pull me off my route, sometimes by only a few hundred yards, sometimes by several miles. Each will build extra time into the ride, a leisurely gift of reflection and appreciation dropped into my day. Here at the first of these covered bridges, I find myself spending a good deal of time poking around the old structure, appreciating both the bridge and the history it represents along this old highway.

Making my way through Greenup, I continue along the flat National Road, farmland stretching out on either side of me, broken up now and then by woodlots or small stands of forest. This is the vast wilderness that was cleared and drained to make way for western agriculture—the dream of the National Road. I've adjusted my pace to accommodate the quartering headwind, and have settled into a pleasant grind down the highway when I see another cyclist coming the other way along the highway. A big smile paints itself across my face and my mood lifts as I find myself relishing a little roadside communion with a fellow traveler.

MARY AND FRIENDS

*The real voyage of discovery consists not in
seeking new landscapes, but in having new eyes.*

Marcel Proust

Mary is a young gal who's cycling from Annapolis to Denver.
For some reason I don't understand, the serendipity of this
doesn't seem all that wild to me. I'm from Denver, cycling to
Annapolis, and out here in the middle of Illinois I meet this
young woman who's cycling from Annapolis to Denver.

Mary has just finished a stint of service in the Peace
Corps, and is headed home to Colorado to spend time with
her folks. She's camping part of the time, so is schlepping a
lot more gear on her bike than I have on mine. She's having
the version of this adventure that fits a 25-year-old, while I'm
having the version of this adventure that a 60-year-old wants.

Her story feels like there might be some *coming of age*
components to life right now, and maybe this cycling trip is part
of that. Recently completed big milestones in life, an arduous
journey across the country back home, maybe the journey is
part of her transition into the next chapter of life. Maybe it's

her way of discovering the next chapter, or at least figuring out which direction to look.

We talk a lot about routes, and I give her my best advice for roads she should consider or not, while she does the same for me. We hang out and chat for a bit, exchange email addresses, then head on down the road.

I'm excited to have met and chatted with a fellow cyclist, still enjoying the little high of shared sojourner's camaraderie, when I spot what might be another cyclist coming toward me on the road. I stop and wait for him at the top of a little rise, trying to put the image together as he slowly makes his way up the hill. It looks like a five-gallon bucket, with a bicycle strapped to the back of it, a melee of miscellany hung and banded together on all sides, creating a two-wheeled behemoth.

Standing on the pedals and coaxing the beast up the hill is a young fella who looks remarkably like a hippie of sorts. Ethan has a friendly wave, and pulls over to chat. Soon after comes his buddy Justin, followed a few minutes later by Morgan. They're all on similar machines, dressed in ragged loose clothes, big smiles on their faces.

My new hippie friends are headed to Colorado as well, though they've just begun their journey in Indianapolis. We chat a bit, and I tell them about Mary who's just a few miles in front of them. Mary's traveling faster than these folks are, and I suggest that surely they must have met her as she passed them not long ago.

"No man, we didn't," Ethan says sheepishly, "we just got on the road a couple of miles ago. We stayed in a campground last night, and got kinda a late start this morning."

Justin and Morgan snicker and exchange a knowing look with each other, and see me noticing. I smile, "A little too much libation maybe?"

Morgan shakes her head, and says, "Not really. I suppose we drank a little and smoked a little, but mostly we were just playing music."

"Yeah," Justin throws in, "we met some really cool folks

in the campground with instruments, and you know how it is, pretty soon the sun's almost up and you're still jammin'. You know?"

Actually I don't. They were just finding their pillows when I was enjoying breakfast with Nancy earlier today, 70 miles behind me. They were probably just thinking about supper last night about the time I was drifting off to sleep. However, not wanting to seem too much the old fogey, I roll my head around in a kind of a nod and shrug my shoulders, hoping they take this as an "oh yeah of course—who doesn't know what that's like?"

"So where you guys hoping to get to tonight?" I ask, trying to get back onto more comfortable ground.

Ethan, who seems to be the logistics coordinator, answers. "We're not sure, man. I guess we'll ride 'til we tire out for the day and find a campground. Are there any campgrounds back the way you came?"

I think about this, realizing that I haven't been paying any attention. Looking back down the road behind me, squinting my eyes as if I could see way back down there from here, I say, "Not really. But then I haven't been paying attention, either."

Ethan and Justin are both gazing back down the road with me, clearly able to see exactly nothing, just like me. I look over at Morgan, who's looking at the three of us like we're stuffin' Play-Doh into our mouths. She smiles when she sees me seeing her seeing us, and adds, "I doubt if we'll be riding very far today. We kind of need a good night's sleep."

I smile as both boys are nodding their heads vigorously. Really, they can't be five miles into the day, and they've already got an eye open for a place to end the day. It's gonna be a long way to Colorado at this rate. I'm curious about their route, so I ask, "what route are you guys taking from here to Colorado?"

Everybody looks at each other and shrugs in unison. Ethan, the logistics coordinator, elaborates. "We're just takin' it as it comes, man. We get there when we get there, and we'll take whatever route seems best at the time."

Morgan and Justin nod and smile. This is clearly a practiced mantra. I'm really taking a shine to these three. They've fashioned bikes out of old clunker machines and duct-taped five-gallon buckets or milk crates onto their handlebars. They've got sleeping bags roped to the backs of their bikes, with fiddles or mandolins tied on top wherever they can. They've struck out toward the mythic mountains in Colorado to discover life and make some music along the way.

Some might call them modern-day hippies on the modern-day version of the VW microbus. Long hair, ragged clothes, maybe the sweet smell of something smoked wafting from them. Unbidden, a vision of *Grapes of Wrath* creeps into my mind as we talk.

I prefer to think of them as true pilgrims, sojourning their way down the highway, whimsical and eccentric for sure, but built on a solid spirit of substantial exploration. Fearless or feckless? Courageous or reckless? Carefree or foolhardy? Tomato or tomahto?

We talk for a bit about routes, and I give them my best advice. They've heard of the Katy Trail, and I encourage them to ride on it, relating my stories of shared music along the trail. I'd love to stand here and get to know these wanderers better, but I can see that they're restless and want to get down the road. Enough jawin' with the weird old guy. We snap a couple of pictures as we part, and I wish them the best.

Really. They're gonna need it . . .

Watching them meander down the road, my first thought is that there's no way they'll make it. Ill-prepared for an arduous journey and riding old clunker bikes that aren't maintained and will probably break down in many ways. They know nothing about how to fix them or take care of them. Their clothes flap in the wind and get caught in bicycle parts. They start riding in the middle of the day when the wind is high, and will be lucky to make 30 or 40 miles a day. They have no route planned or mapped, and no idea where they'll stop each day.

I'm transfixed by the scene, watching them rolling down the road into the west. The breeze is pushing them along just a little bit, which is a tiny fraction of the good fortune they need. I'm dazzled by their courage, enchanted by their innocence. Cojones. Real cojones.

We're all on our own version of life's journey. Figuratively, metaphorically, and literally. We all have different notions of what we might find on the journey, why we're there, and how we travel. Whether it's a bike ride across the country or our drive to work in the morning, every step is a segment of the journey we're assembling into the thing we call life.

Mary pedals purposefully toward Colorado along her well-planned route with youthful determination. She prepared herself for a journey, packed well for it, and is making her way methodically across the country. She'll find her next purpose. When she gets to Colorado to spend time with her folks, I can picture conversations where they share big dreams and ideas, and plan ways to make that happen.

Ethan, Justin, and Morgan are on the same road with Mary, just a few miles back. (Well, by now Mary has gained a few more miles on them . . .) Their target isn't as pinpointed as Mary's, or their route as well thought-out; they just know they need to keep chasing the setting sun. They're gonna find something, and have adventures, and be happy. They're all young, chasing the future, the bulk of their days ahead, the middle of life not even in view yet.

Spokes and wheels. Watching their slow progress as they ride away, images of spokes and wheels keep turning through my mind. The wheels of our lives rolled past each other out here on the Old National Road today. Different spokes make up our varied histories, and have led us each to this point of intersection along the road. The degree to which those spokes overlap—both in the past and in the expected future—fascinates me. Mary began at my destination city, and is headed to a place just a few miles from my home. Ethan, Justin, and

Morgan making their way methodically and musically toward some as-yet unknown destination in my home state. Serendipity. Again.

As my new sojourner friends disappear over a distant hill, I turn my back and climb into the saddle, coasting down a little hill, turning the cranks as I start to go up, finding that steady cadence I like so much. A sense of good fortune overwhelms me as my legs find a familiar steady rhythm. I'm nearly at the end of my sixth decade, and I'm only surviving a ride like this thanks to a lot of physical preparation. But at this point in life, that physical preparation is a big part of the journey itself.

I remember a time when setting out in a direction and seeing where the winds would blow me was an adventure. These days, I've come to understand that the planning gnomes in my tiny little brain are comforted by a solid map and direction. I might waver from that map now and then, but the fact that it's there brings me comfort.

For me, right now, this doesn't really feel like a journey of discovery. Maybe something more akin to fulfillment. Or attainment. Or contentment.

Most of us struggle to find the joy in the present moment. It would be easy to look at the indomitable spirit of these young folks I just met, and remember longingly that time when more road was in front of me than behind. That time of young adventure, looking for worlds to conquer. That time of misadventure when my body was built for sleeping on cold hard ground and launching into hardship half prepared. Those distant moments of hippie-ness in my own experience, in pursuit of distant and seemingly achievable idealistic nirvana.

But this moment—right here, right now—is a different moment for me. A moment I'm relishing with every ounce of me. I'm still headed toward a destination, and still have aspirations. They're just different now. More relaxed I suppose. More comfortable.

I like where I am, and where I feel like I'm going. The spokes stretching out in front of me are connected to the ones that got me here by the hub that is the here and now. While it's impossible to predict where I'll go along this wheel of life, there's comfort in seeing the path behind reflected in likely paths ahead.

I'm a happy man. Smiling, enjoying the warmth of familiar cadence coursing through my legs.

Pedal, breathe, smile, and enjoy.

A LITTLE SOMETHING EXTRA

*Spread love everywhere you go. Let no one
ever come to you without leaving happier.*

Mother Teresa

DAY 30 • TERRE HAUTE TO INDIANAPOLIS, INDIANA

The biggest downside of the west-to-east direction I'm following across the country is that every morning at sunrise, I'm riding into the sun. Not that this bothers me much on the bike, but it puts me at much greater risk as the drivers approaching from behind are likely to have impaired vision from the bright sun.

This morning that danger feels acute as I ride in the heavy traffic headed east out of downtown Terra Haute. The sun is bright and low, directly in front of me, making it very likely that drivers approaching from behind don't see me until the last minute. I'd hoped to get further down the road before eating breakfast, but instead pull into a little diner, hoping to let the sun get a little higher before getting back on the road.

There at the diner, I wallow in the comfort of good breakfast fare. A plate covered in hash browns, chicken-fried steak spilling over the edge, eggs layered on top of the steak, bacon laying across the eggs. American breakfast. Digging into the feast, I realize that these diner breakfast debaucheries are one of the high points of this journey. I could never afford the calories in this breakfast were it not for the upcoming miles on the bike.

The waitress is classic. Slightly friendly, spread too thinly across too many tables, she knows her business like a pro. My coffee cup is never empty, and my water glass gets filled every time it gets low. She takes my plate as soon as I've scrubbed the final crumb from it. Nothing fancy, a welcome absence of catchy responses; just down-home friendly service that's good.

In a diner like this, it's pretty common that I'll leave a $5 tip for this kind of service. The breakfast tab might have only been $10, but there's some level of affinity I have with the folks who work their tails off in diners, and they're working hard for the tips they earn.

As I count out the money to leave for her on the table, enough to cover the tab plus an extra $5, I wonder about my motivations for tipping. Last night at the somewhat fancy restaurant with a bar where I ate in downtown Terra Haute, the young waitress was so engrossed in the television show playing on the set behind that bar that I had to get up and get her when I wanted to order. I noticed the couple at the table next to me getting pretty aggravated at the service void they were feeling as well. I fumed about the situation as I tried to enjoy my supper, and ended up leaving a tip, albeit a small one.

I'm not crazy about the way our dining culture operates when it comes to how we treat waitstaff. The enterprise who hires them pays them next to nothing, as the minimum wage laws allow exceptions for people who earn tips. So they're heavily dependent on tips. The dining public not only has to pay for their meal, but is also expected to pay the dining establishment's wage costs in the form of a tip.

The norm these days seems to be that dining establishments understaff. It's a balance, because the waitstaff doesn't want overstaffing, which limits the number of tables they serve.

But understaffing often results in poor service, and the waiter is the one whose earnings suffer from poor service. Other cultures have a different model, where the restaurant owner pays well enough to maintain good staff. In the case of exceptional service, I might leave a little something, but it's not an expected source of income for the waiter; it's more like a bonus.

Hey, I'm all for the free market and entrepreneurship and all that, but it's got to be applied across the board. We can't decide that it's only the waitstaff whose income is defined by the quality of the product, the service received, and the mood of the customer. It should be all or nothing. What if I don't like the way the meal is prepared, or don't like the ambiance of the place? Do I get to decide to pay less for my meal? Sure, the check says I owe $28, but the food was only average, and the place is noisy, so I think I'll just pay $5 today. Watch as I get handcuffed walking out the door.

Last night was an exception, in that the waitress *chose* to ignore her tables. Her tip from me reflected that choice. This morning was an exception, in that I feel an affinity toward my diner waitress, and appreciate her hard work and dedication. She's trying hard to make a living, and I want to help. It's probably selfish as much as it is benevolent, since it makes me feel good to leave it.

Smiling as I walk out the front door, I tell the waitress thanks, and wish her a great day. Climbing into the saddle, I'm relieved to see a little midwestern haze in the sky reducing the glare of the sun, which has climbed enough now that I feel more safe on the road.

COVERED BRIDGES

*In rivers, the water that you touch is the last
of what has passed and the first of that which
comes; so with present time.*

Leonardo da Vinci

Today is an easy riding day, with something less than 75 miles planned. I take the time to explore the many little spurs off of US 40, representing the old iterations of the National Road. Many of these involve ancient and cracked pavement that is either abandoned or has become a rarely used access path to a field or barn. A couple of times I find myself exploring old bridge structures as they languish in silence, draped in trees and vines, a few hundred yards from the newer version of the highway.

I've also programmed a couple of covered bridge locations into my Garmin, and the beautiful weather has me in an exploring mood. The route to the bridges takes me many miles north of US 40, but it's worth the detour.

There's something magical in an old covered bridge. The Houck Bridge and the Oakalla/Shoppell Bridge both cross the Big Walnut Creek, and I'm pulled into a little moment of enchantment as I explore first one then the other. My mind appreciates the engineering that's apparent in the structures, but the mellow strength of the old structures plays to my heart. The quiet of the remote countryside, broken only by the trickle of the creek below, intoxicates me and holds my soul close.

The bridges speak of a culture that cared about doing things well, about doing things in a way that lasts. Even the design concept—covering a bridge to be sure the creek can be crossed even in deep snow and ice—speaks of a culture bound and determined to live life fully day and night, every day of the year.

These bridges cross a small creek deep in rural Indiana, and to say traffic is light would be an understatement. I see two cars in the hour or so I spend poking around these old pearls. I'm grateful for the solitude on such a lovely day in an enchanting setting.

Leaning out to watch the creek flowing gently below me, the Japanese phrase *wabi-sabi* comes to mind. The phrase has evolved in meaning over the centuries—as words or phrases often do—today coming to represent a complex harmony between simplicity, humility, imperfection, and the caress of time on all things. The phrase speaks to me as I feel the solid planks under my feet, hear the simple voice of practicality in the design, and feel the age in the ancient worn wood. Simple, clean, strong, worn. Loved. Cared-for.

A beautiful fall day drifts around me. The tranquility of the moment captures me. I'd like to take a nap and spend the rest of the day here. But I need to be in Indy this evening at a decent hour to share supper with an old friend. That balance again. Giving myself to the enjoyment of the moment while acknowledging the little planning gnomes and schedule trolls that are clearly part of me.

I walk my bike slowly along the old planks of the Oakalla Bridge, then climb into the saddle and begin meandering down the gravel road that will take me back toward the modern world of pavement. I've barely begun turning the pedals when I notice a pair of fawns playing in the road 100 yards in front of me. I stop to watch, as they don't seem to perceive my bicycle with me on it to be much of a threat.

At any other time, in any other circumstance, the fawns might be less fascinating to me. But right here, in this moment of nostalgic appreciation of a time and place when we cared more than we do today about building things that last, I find the playful antics of the fawns to be a perfect amplification to the quiet constancy of the bridge behind me.

The fawns are given completely to the simple joy of the moment. After ten minutes or so of play, something shiny catches their attention, and they bounce off into the timber that runs between the creek and the road. Their time here is measured in a few short years, and they capture each moment as it comes to them. Behind me, the bridge lives in a moment that's measured in centuries, and it becomes a part of each moment that trickles past it.

A couple of miles of gravel leads to an old county road on the outskirts of the college town of Greencastle. I realize, as I pedal into town and around the quaint old town square, that college students here probably make their way the few miles out to the Oakalla Bridge on autumn weekends to enjoy in the way college students enjoy remote places in the woods.

You know, for the history.

My memory slips back the decades in time to my years in college, and summer days when I'd make my way out to the swimming holes and shady spots along the creek with friends. I find myself remembering one day in particular, an afternoon spent with a girl I was sweet on, wandering through the Kansas hills around the small college town we lived in.

This was the same girl we met earlier in this story. The one who'd whup on me on the tennis court. The one I'd share ice cream with at Baskin-Robbins after she whupped on me. The one I was too shy to ask out on a more formal date. But on a wonderful summer day, she jumped on the back of my motorcycle with me, and we had an afternoon of adventure together.

A splendid day spent in a lovely setting with a beautiful girl. We explored the rolling hills, and found a wonderful spot along a quiet sparkling creek, deep in the woods. An enchanted day spent falling in love with someone, spinning that magical web of enchantment that's young and new, a rich concoction boiling with delight and tenderness and timidness and lust and wonder.

But then life happens, and timing isn't quite right, and that one beautiful day together fades into our memory. I suppose most folks have a memory that's something like that. The stars all lined up, and briefly filled our hearts with an epic sense of romance and love, then life shuffled us on down a different road. Some combination of things not said or opportunities not grasped.

My road through life has been filled with adventure and love and delight. I'm lucky and grateful for the wonderful journey I've had, and the remarkable people who've been part of that sojourn. I've shuffled now through nearly six decades, and find myself exploring new roads and finding new adventure.

Rolling through this quintessential small midwestern college town, that time of magic all those decades ago is bumping up against my recollection. The pleasant memory fills me as I tool along the little streets. Some cocktail of sweet memories stirred together with regret and hope play with my emotions beneath the warm September sunshine.

Her name was Christine.

As it turns out, I've bumped into Christine again online recently. Preparing for the last day of riding on this trip, I struggled to find the route that would work best through or around D.C. I was having trouble getting good advice, and I started digging through friends of friends on Facebook, looking for someone who lived in the D.C. area who might be a cyclist. I found a friend of a friend who lived not far from D.C., recognized the picture as Christine, and wrote for advice. We hadn't had any contact in over 30 years, and I wondered if her memory of me was as endearing as my memory of her.

"Of course," she had written. "I remember well." We fell into a familiar conversation as if there weren't decades between this conversation and the last. "Funny you should get in contact with me at this point, though."

"Oh yeah, why's that?"

"Well, I ended a 30-year marriage not long ago, and I just think it's interesting that this would be the time you'd contact me."

"Hmmm. I ended a 30-year marriage not long ago too. I guess that *is* interesting. This contact made any earlier than right now would have been very different, wouldn't it?"

"Indeed it would have been. And our timing was never that good, was it?"

"It wasn't."

"When did you say you'll be out here?"

And so it went. We'll connect on the east coast when I complete this ride.

Synchronicity.

SHUTTERING GREMLINS

Remorse is the poison of life.

Charlotte Bronte, *Jane Eyre*

Shouldering through a crowded bakery section at the Almost Home Restaurant right off the Greencastle town square, I settle in to the only empty table in the café. Having slipped my reading glasses on, I'm perusing the menu when someone touches me on the shoulder.

"Excuse me, but there aren't any empty tables—would you mind terribly if I joined you?" The words have a very slight Australian accent, simply adorable coming from the attractive young woman whose hand still rests on my shoulder.

Hey, it's a small town, and folks are just probably really friendly here. In a different setting, this would be overtly flirtatious behavior, but here in the little café in the tiny midwestern college town, she's just looking for a place to sit and enjoy lunch. And who could resist that accent?

"Of course," I exclaim as I stand and move my helmet from the table and make room for her. "This is a crowded place!"

"The food's bonza, isn't it? It's the best place around for lunch."

"I'll take your word for it—I'm just passin' through. But it smells great! I'm Neil, by the way."

"Nice to meet you Neil, I'm Ann." She smiles broadly and reaches her hand toward me, placing it in mine in that sensual way women can do; not really limp, but soft and gentle. Responsive. "So you're on a bicycle but you don't live here? Where did you ride from?"

I give her the 30-second version of the trip, and watch her facial expression morph into that *oh wow* look that some folks get when they hear the story. She pulls back slightly while exclaiming, "Fair dinkum, mate!"

I assume this is some sort of Aussie expression that expresses amazement. Or it may be Aussie for something akin to *you big fat liar*. Regardless of how she means it, I choose to take it as something like, *oh wow Neil, what a big strong man you are*. While I'd normally respond to this with an *aw shucks, it's nothin'* reply, because really it just feels like pedaling a bike and having fun, I make a split second decision that there are some situations where it's best to just go with the flow. Like when it's a pretty young woman doing the *oh wow*-ing or the *fair dinkum*-ing.

Is this how rock stars feel? And how does this happen anyway? We're such predictable creatures, with such predictably irrational behavior. I love feeling *ow wow*ed by her, and her smile tells me she enjoys doing the *oh wow*ing and enjoys the fact that it has such an impact on me.

"So where did you start this morning, and where will you end tonight?"

I pause for a second, enjoying how her accent turns the word "tonight" into the word "tonoit.

"Started in Terra Haute this morning, and I'll end up just outside Indy tonight."

Her eyebrows crinkle with a question, her head turning slightly. She opens her mouth to speak, then pauses, and I notice just how attractive her mouth is when she pauses. My predictability irritates me. Then she speaks with that somewhat dry Aussie humor. "Neil, you may actually be a bit lost, then. There's a road that runs directly between those two places, and woop woop here out in the middle of nowhere isn't on that road. I feel it's my responsibility to tell you this before you pedal any further."

I chuckle with her as I assimilate this new woop woop expression, which I figure must be more Aussie for something like a small town, appreciating her transformation of the word "my" into the word "moiy." I explain that I've planned for a relatively short day today, so figured I had time to detour up this way to explore a couple of old covered bridges outside town.

I realize after I say this that the notion of detouring just to see some old covered bridges exposes the "just a romantic" side of me, which she seems to find attractive. The adoration positively sparkles from her eyes. I make a note to check out the help-wanted ads for rock stars. It would take zero time for me to adapt to this.

The waitress takes our order. I go with a nice salad since this is a light calorie burn day and both breakfast and dinner are big meals for me today.

Ann comments on the order. "Not much tucker for somebody riding their bike so far." She sees the confusion on my face, and continues, "Oh sorry mate—I keep using Aussie slang, don't I? I mean that's not much food."

I realize that my earlier somewhat romanticized comments about detouring from the bike ride just to see some old covered bridges, paired with ordering a salad for lunch, and spiced with the healthy dose of spandex I'm wrapped in, don't make for a very manly image. While I perceive attraction from Ann, I realize that it's clearly attraction toward the idea of riding across the country on a bike, not toward me.

I'm okay with that.

While my mind knows that her comment is rhetorical and requires no response, my fragile male ego demands that an explanation be given. "I'm meeting an old friend for dinner tonight in Indy, and I had a really big breakfast. Plus the salad just sounds good."

"Good choice. They've the best Cobb salad I've ever tasted. You'll love it." She pauses, unrolling her silverware and placing her napkin in her lap very softly, her eyes following the movement of her hands, lingering there, then bringing her eyes up to look back at me. This is the place where I get really clumsy in conversations that feel like flirting, and I mostly default to being quiet. "So tell me about dinner tonight. This is a mate you've known a long time?"

"A long time. My wife and I were good friends with her and her husband when we all lived in Ohio. We went to church together. We watched each other's kids growing up together. But we moved away from Ohio 15 years ago, and I think they moved away about the same time."

Her body language changes noticeably, and as I finish the sentence I realize that "married" is probably not a flirting word. Have I mentioned before just how much I suck at this flirting thing?

"So you're married? How does your wife feel about you riding across the country?"

"Well I *was* married, but I'm divorced now. But my ex-wife was really supportive of the ride. We're good friends."

I stop talking, realizing that I'm just not good at this. But Ann has leaned back into the conversation. "Dinner with long-lost mates can be cracker. Well at least usually. Sometimes it can be the dog's breakfast, depending on where the conversation goes." She looks at me and cocks her head slightly, a meaningful look on her face. "Know what I mean?"

Why are Aussie accents so fascinating? I love the way "usually" becomes some elongated form with a couple of long Us: on the front, an extra U in the middle, a strong emphasis on the first syllable, and a huge underline beneath the whole word.

"I think so. Assuming *cracker* means great and *dog's breakfast* means bad, right?"

"Oh right. So sorry. But yeah, that's what those things mean. I mean, some folks are always looking back in a way that over-romanticizes the past, and assumes yesterday was always better than today. Right?"

There's some more of it—turning "right" into "roit." My fascination with her accent almost makes it hard to concentrate. But I muster an answer. "You bet. Always looking backwards with rose-colored glasses, too focused on trying to figure out why today can't be as good as yesterday was."

"Now there's a Yank phrase I need to pick up and start using—*you bet*. I like it! And you're on it exactly, yesterday wasn't always all that good. We just remember the good stuff."

"Well, not always. Don't you think there are folks who look back with more regret than positive nostalgia?"

"Good point. Maybe that's a defining feature of our personalities. A glass half-full or half-empty thing."

"So Ann, which camp do you fall into? Is the past a rose-colored utopia or a regret-filled miasma?"

She pauses, looking at me meaningfully, seemingly pleased to be asked. "Oh I reckon my rose-colored glasses are fully functional! I don't believe in regrets. What's in the past, is in the past, good or bad." She fiddles with her fork, lining it up more precisely with her knife and spoon, then continues. "Remembering the bad stuff doesn't help us be happy today, so I choose to remember the good stuff. I want to be happy today."

"Kind of like today is the corner between yesterday and tomorrow? How we view the past helps define the corner we're turning into the future?"

"Well yeah, that's a great way to say it."

"But still, that doesn't mean we don't have regrets, right? No offense, but there's a difference between having no regrets and casting our regrets aside and forgetting about them."

After the words leave my mouth I realize that I probably appear to be trying to start an argument with this woman I just met. I've heard folks say this before—that they have no regrets—and I always have such a hard time reconciling the statement with real life. However, when she answers, Ann seems genuinely into the conversation and not at all put off by the challenge.

"Maybe it's semantics. I reckon I've made choices in life that I'd make differently if given the chance. I accept that, and hopefully I learned from the bad choices. There are lots of things I'd do differently if we got *do-overs*. But are those *regrets?*"

"That's how I'm using the word anyway. A regret is something I'd like to do differently than I did—something I'd like a *do-over* on, to use your phrase."

"But you're in a good place in life, right? Here you are cycling across the country, carefree, loving life. Surely you don't regret where you are, or wish you were somewhere else, right? Even those things you'd like a *do-over* on, didn't some good come out of your choices, even when they weren't the best of choices?"

"Well sure. And I think you've hit on the difference in the way we're using the word. There's almost always good that we can find in any situation. And I *don't* wish I were somewhere else or in a different situation. If that's your definition of regrets, then I agree with you, and I don't *regret* where I am or how I got here."

"Well there you are then!" Ann sits back with a delightful smile, eyes bright and shining with triumph, just as our waitress arrives with lunch. We survey the fare, then Ann says something about *tucking in* as I continue the thought out loud.

"But I *do* regret certain things I've said or done, or *not said* or *not done*. It seems like you agree that we all have those things, right?"

"Well of course," she dismisses with a wave of her fork. "But what do you want your life to be defined by, Neil—the things you regret or the things you're delighted with?"

Delight. I love that word. It says so much. I smile at her use of it, and give a tiny shrug and nod to acknowledge that she's right in what she's saying. My mouth is full so I can't really answer, and she continues.

"In those moments when I'm completely honest with myself, I admit that there are times when something from my past peeks 'round the corner at me in a way I don't like. It's almost always some little thing I said, or failed to say, and I desperately want that moment back to fix what I said wrong. Sometimes it's things I did or didn't do, but I think more often it's words rather than deeds."

"And do those moments bring just a tiny shudder from inside? A revulsion?"

"Yes! Exactly! Just a fleeting little moment of disgust that I didn't have the courage to say what needed to be said, or said something I shouldn't have. And really, it *does* feel like a shudder!"

"Yeah, I get that too. Not often, but sometimes. A dark shadow trying to steal fragments of joy from the moment I'm in."

"Like a little gremlin reminding you that you might not be as good as you think you are, making you shudder at the realization."

"Perfect! Shuddering gremlins. Yeah I suppose it feels like that. And do you think that the gremlin is better at remembering the things you *did* that you wish you didn't, or the things you *didn't do* that you wish you did?"

Ann stops and thinks about this while she chews. A couple of times she starts to speak but stops before answering. "Now that's a great question. I've heard it said that it's the things we fail to do that we regret, but I'm not sure I agree. I mean, there are surely things I've done that I wish I hadn't done."

She turns the word "surely" into "shooorly," underlined strongly. Really, having a conversation with someone who has an accent like this is akin to exploring a foreign language.

"Yep, I've heard the same thing before, and likewise I'm not sure I agree. But maybe this is the place to parse the meaning of that word *regret*. Because the word regret does seem to feel like a better description of those things I *didn't do or say* that I *wish I would have done or said.* I'm just not sure what the right word is for the things I did or said but wish I hadn't."

"It's a pretty fine distinction, but I agree. The word *regret* best describes things I failed to do." She's nodding, gazing out the window, thinking. "Now what word would describe the other thing? Maybe something like annoyance?"

"Maybe, but not strong enough. Anguish? Remorse?"

"Self-reproach?"

I nod and smile. "Like a slap on the hand. One is anger, one is sadness."

"That's it! I feel mad at myself for stupid things I did or choices I made, but sorrowful over the things I failed to say or do."

"One of the world's problems solved, right here at the lunch table in Greencastle, Indiana."

She raises her water glass to toast. "Good on us! Cheers, mate!"

"Cheers!"

Later, turning the pedals on my bike and making my way toward Indy, I ponder the depth to which we sometimes open up to a complete stranger. I don't think I'd ever discussed the shuddering gremlin thing with anyone else in life, but here in woop woop America, in a crowded café with a woman I just met, I come to understand that I'm not the only person in the world who's met these thieving little monsters.

Strangers in our life—at least the right strangers—are probably as important in many ways as our friends. We have no long-term attachment to them, no long-term impression to build or maintain. We can let more of our deep self show than we can with the people in our life who'll continue to matter. We can let our hair hang down just a little more, and maybe let them catch glimpses into us that we usually hide.

TRIBAL EQUITY

It's the great mystery of human life that old grief passes gradually into quiet tender joy.

Fyodor Dostoevsky, *The Brothers Karamazov*

From where I sit in life, the meaning of the phrase *old friend* has begun to take on two meanings. Tonight I find myself having dinner with a friend whom I knew many years ago, who is also (like me) getting old.

Age is such a fluid thing, isn't it? When I was 10, someone who was 20 seemed quite old. Now at nearly 60, someone who's 20 seems like a child to me. Old is x+10, where x is your current age. Nonetheless, I find that the dear friend I'm sharing supper with tonight looks across the table at me with eyes that hint of wrinkles of wisdom, wrinkles similar to the ones I see in the eyes that stare back at me from the mirror.

Wabi-sabi. Worn by life. Imperfect, having earned a value that could only have been achieved by the path taken, the miles traveled, the mistakes made, the joy inhaled.

I've known Cathy for nearly 30 years. Our children played together when they were very small. Cathy and her husband

Larry and their children, along with my ex-wife and I and our children, spent many Sunday afternoons or Saturday evenings together. We hosted Passover Seders together. But jobs changed, and people moved, and friendships developed distance.

Larry is traveling this week, so only Cathy could join me tonight. Years ago, Cathy and I would often engage in lively debates that involved politics and/or religion. Our positions on topics were rarely the same, and we respected each other enough to have frisky disputation that was very friendly. I'm hopeful that tonight holds some of that sort of discussion, along with reminiscence of old friendship.

But instead, foolishly unexpectedly, I find that we're going to mourn together. We'll mourn the loss of a marriage. My marriage.

I'm a very private person, as is the woman I was married to for 30 years. When we decided to get divorced, we didn't talk about it with anyone else. We went about the task in a very businesslike fashion, as we did most things in our relationship. Our discussion about the topic with our grown children occurred after the divorce was final.

Our children were surprised, though maybe not shocked. Many people, though, were shocked. I was dismayed at their shock. This was our business, and our business alone. We needed to deal with this on our own, and move on in life. To me, divorce was a process that was painful, hurtful, filled with regret, and very private.

But I was wrong. I handled divorce very poorly, and this becomes apparent to me in what I feel from Cathy as we share a supper.

Cathy is devastated by this news, and her anger at me is apparent. There's zero logic in this to me, which keeps me rocking on my heels, unable to converse intelligently. How can she be so devastated and angry? This was my marriage that came unwound over time, and eventually dissolved. This is a pain I went through with the woman I was married to and loved for so many years. It seems to me that Cathy should be sympathetic and consoling, not angry.

It'd be easy for me to be glib here, and toss this off with humor about the difference between logic and emotion. Humor lets me justify my callousness, and hide behind my analytical nature. Logic is easy. It makes sense to me. I suppose that's why I hide there so often.

Humans might be capable of logic, but we're driven by emotion. And somewhere this evening things have gone terribly awry, far from the safe boundaries of logic, spinning chaotically in the universe of emotion. There is little discussion that feels to me anything like reminiscence. There's no joy at a conversation with an old friend. There's only anger and grief.

It will take me a long time to process and understand the dynamic of my discussion with Cathy, to feel what's really happening beneath the surface. When I do, I think it will be something like this:

Marriage isn't a private union between two people. It's a public thing. It's shared equity in the complex web of human tribal glue. Often, it's the key and primary glue. When a marriage unwinds, it takes with it threads that reach deep into the many layers of friendships, family, and other relationships that make up our life and define our tribe.

I know that in some ways, our selfish 20th-century culture cheapened marriage with easy divorce. There are lots of folks who'd like to ignore the complexity of the situation by labeling this cheapening with some moniker that's two syllables or less and will attract voters. I know many folks who want to throw around words like "sanctity" and "sacredness," who want marriage to be a really simple thing that matches their own bias.

Marriage *is* a sacred thing, but not in the way politicians like to throw around. It's not a religious thing in general, though it may be to some individuals. To our culture as a whole, it's sacred because it's a key cement that holds the tribe together. When two people choose to intertwine their lives together in the public declaration of a marriage union, the tribe is strengthened by the glue the union brings.

It doesn't matter who the two people are, or what color their skin is, or what altar they worship at. It doesn't matter what gender they are, or what political party they belong to. What matters is the public declaration of love and union. It's tribal equity. Unwinding the union is a loss to the tribe—to everybody around the couple, not just to the couple themselves.

I'm typing these words, understanding more about Cathy's anger, and about her *right* to mourn the loss of my marriage. To Cathy: *I understand now, and I'm sorry.*

We finish supper, and I say good-bye to Cathy. The pain in the tears I see in her eyes cuts me deeply. I don't think I've ever been very good at making relationships work, and I see now that this probably has a lot to do with my lack of emotional intelligence when it comes to things like this. I climb the stairs to my motel room and fall into the sheets, hoping for a good night's sleep.

My thoughts drift back to my discussion with Ann earlier in the day. This deep sorrow inside me right now is nothing like the shuddering gremlins, but is exactly the definition of *regret* that we talked about. It's a sorrow that fills me down into my bones over my failure to make a relationship work with someone I loved.

I suppose some breakups are different, in that they're about things we do that we wish we hadn't. In those cases, maybe they feel the shuddering gremlins more than the deep sorrow. My marriage failure isn't about things done, but about things not done.

A relationship between two people will grow into a thing itself as it develops. It becomes more than just a point of intersection. It becomes an emotional organism in and of itself. Tribal equity that requires care and feeding. Each one is different, with its own set of needs and wants, but they all need nurturing. No matter how much attraction brings two people together, no matter how much chemistry they feel, no matter how right it feels at the beginning, they both have to commit themselves to a life as a shepherd of the relationship itself, or it will eventually wither. We all have to find ways to help one another to be good shepherds of relationships if we don't want to lose that tribal equity.

My thoughts are disrupted as I realize I'm sweating in the sheets. A disclaimer here: my standards for motel rooms are pretty low. I require very little. I generally don't sleep much anyway, so a really nice room is a bit of a waste on me. All I require is a relatively clean room, and quiet. One or the other, and I'm probably good for the night.

Tonight I have neither. The sweating, it turns out, is because there's a layer of plastic between the sheet and the mattress. I don't think I want to know why motel management finds this necessary. Angry, I strip the plastic off the bed, and crawl back into the sheets after making the bed up again, sans the plastic protection.

I'm drifting right up against the edge of sleep, when the couple in the room next to me start yelling at each other. The walls are thin. Really thin. At first I hope the fight will end soon, and nobody will get hurt. But it doesn't end, it escalates. Now I'm getting worried that somebody will get hurt. But the tone starts to evolve, and I realize that what I'm listening to is rapidly moving from the sounds of fighting to the sounds of foreplay. My new hope is that the foreplay won't last long. It doesn't. What comes after lasts even less time.

So there. We got that out of our system. Now let's all settle down and get some sleep.

Just as I'm rocking up against that shore of sleep, I'm disturbed by the sounds of raucous laughter and fun, this time from a bunch of bikers with rooms not far away. This, unfortunately, lasts much longer than the fight/foreplay/fast-finish that kept me awake a little bit ago, and I resign myself to a lousy night's sleep.

Lying awake, listening to the good-natured laughter of folks sharing a couple of beers together, hanging out on their bikes outside the room, I find myself enjoying the friendship and camaraderie in the voices I hear. As much as I enjoy solitude and time alone, I'm coming to understand more about the sacredness of relationships, the sanctity of deep and lasting relationships to both us as individuals and to the tribes we're part of.

I'm also coming to understand more about the nature of regrets. We live our lives on a balance beam of sorts, always wavering between action and inaction. Take the wrong action, and there's some risk of a shuddering gremlin haunting us now and then. But take no action, and we sow the seeds of regret that will wrap their roots deeply into our lives in ways that are sometimes deep and mournful.

When it comes to relationships that grow into an entity of their own—relationships like marriage—I doubt if inaction is ever the right choice. Nurturing is a choice we need to make, and never stop making.

Energy we need to muster.

Investment we need to make.

Courage we need to find.

Risk we need to take.

Relationships. Bridges between people. My day today has been filled with bridges of many sorts. New bridges to a newfound friend exploring ideas in a brand new way, old bridges with an old friend reaching across the sorrow of a divorce, the regret of bridges that have crumbled.

The beauty of weathered old covered bridges. Well-cared-for structures built carefully and invested in over the years. Solid in spite of the odds. Standing strong, carrying folks safely from one bank to the other, year after year. Still standing true because we value the bridge, and choose action over inaction, attentiveness over neglect.

Wabi-sabi. Beauty and value not *in spite of* imperfections, but *as a result of* those worn spots.

RED HAT LADIES

*Whenever you find yourself on the side of
the majority, it is time to pause and reflect.*

Mark Twain

DAY 31 • INDIANAPOLIS TO RICHMOND, INDIANA

I'm sure my dreams are infested with bed bugs and other worse
things that might be crawling around the room as I struggle
to find sleep. I'm up and out the door well before dawn, es-
caping from the awful room and looking for a place to have
some breakfast.

Today I'll ride about 90 miles to Richmond, where I'll
meet up with Dave again. Earlier in the summer, Dave rode east
from north of Council Grove in Kansas, across the Midwest,
ending up in Richmond, Indiana. He did that ride by himself,
then drove a rental car home. Dave left Colorado yesterday
after work, and has been driving a rental car loaded with his
bike out to Richmond, where we'll reconnect for the final 500
or 600 miles of this journey.

Dave, I realize, is one of those covered bridges in my life.
Solid and true. I'm looking forward to the deep and wide-ranging

conversations we're bound to have as we share suppers together over the next week. In those brief periods when I'm able to keep up with him as we ride, we'll have some conversation on the road as we turn the cranks.

I've enjoyed my time of solitude on this ride, as I always do. Now I'm looking forward to companionship. Alone and together—a symbiotic balance to me. My alone time helps me appreciate the time I spend with friends, and my together time helps me appreciate solitude when I get it. This morning will be my last morning to enjoy the quiet predawn road by myself, and I'm treated to a few brief displays of crimson color in the eastern sky peeking out from beneath a shroud of gray midwestern cloud cover.

Making my way across the south side of Indianapolis by crossing on secondary and suburban roads, I find the going pretty easy, with few places where I feel at risk. Well, no more at risk than any cyclist feels any day on the road with cars and trucks. A light mist falls throughout the morning, occasionally becoming light rain, and again today I face a quartering headwind. The mist and rain is just heavy enough to keep the road damp most of the time. A brief light shower now and then covers my glasses, but it's never enough to soak me through, so long as I continue to work hard enough to generate good heat.

The road becomes increasingly rural as I move out of Indy toward the east, and I'm struck by the preponderance of houses that fly the Confederate flag. Many times, I see a flagpole out in front, flying the Confederate flag on top and another flag beneath, often a state flag. There's even one instance where the Confederate flag flies above the American flag.

Not that I'm a big flag person. I think flags in general can too quickly become overly nationalistic, and overt nationalism (in any flavor) always leads to nasty things, in my opinion. Years ago, as part of a church congregation in Ohio, I watched a struggle between nationalism and religion unfold and resolve in a way that helped me shape my views.

It was that era in the eighties when one of the parties was

working hard to establish itself as the party who loved the flag the most. (Is that era over yet?) Most of the congregation certainly leaned toward that party, and there was a big push to get the American flag up behind the altar as part of the background. Ed, the pastor, resisted the movement, and a power struggle ensued.

Now, I can't tell you whether Pastor Ed was a Republican or a Democrat. He and I were good friends, but he never let his political views be known to anyone in the congregation. What he did make clear was his opinion that politics and nationalism had no place in the church. Ed's religion was deep and old, not tied to a flag or a nation. He believed strongly that trying to let nationalism coattail with religion just whored-up the religion. (My words, not his.)

So he fought that battle, and won. No American flag in church. Some parishioners came from *the left,* and some from *the right.* But in church, Ed made sure we were all spiritual beings seeking spiritual sustenance. He made sure nationalism didn't creep up onto the altar.

I'm remembering Ed and his battle this morning, as I notice all the Confederate flags flying. I'm not a Southerner, so the Confederate flag thing is something I don't understand well. As with all things, there are two sides to the story, and the simple answers are rarely complete answers.

To most folks in America, the Confederate flag is a symbol of some combination of overt racism and a rebellion against what they believe America stands for. Flying that flag, to them, is akin to shouting out that you're a racist, and that you believe the wrong side won the Civil War. In their eyes, America won the Civil War, and the Confederacy lost, so believing the wrong side won is akin to treason. Not to mention their moral objections to the overt racism that slavery represented.

To some who consider themselves Southerners, the flag is a symbol of the rights of individual states to govern themselves. Whether slavery was wrong, or whether racism in general is wrong, isn't what the flag represents. To them, the South as a region is their first loyalty, and they've grown up in a culture that still stings from what they believe was an overstepping federal government defining their laws for them. The flag represents that "first loyalty" to them—their homeland.

A zeal for a homeland lost. Almost religious fervor. In a roundabout way, This is that unhealthy marriage between religion and nationalism that Pastor Ed was concerned about all those years ago.

Hence our continued inability, as Americans, to agree on if, when, or how it's appropriate to display the stars and bars. Passing the occasional flag this morning, I can't help wondering what message the owner hopes to send by flying the flag. Is it their way of remembering what they believe was a good and just cause? Are they just trying to remember the tragedy of the Civil War? Are they trying to make some political statement about states' rights? Are there subtle and implicit racist overtones to their gesture? Are they folks who put the memory of the Confederacy above the reality of today's America, and want to secede?

Who knows why they do it. I suppose someone with hard nationalist leanings would be offended that they fly the stars and bars and ignore the stars and stripes, or worse, fly the bars above the stripes. To me, all it means is that from here to Annapolis, I'll be skirting that line that still exists between North and South in America.

The road has narrowed, and is sparsely traveled. Tall trees arch over the pavement from both sides, defining a long and picturesque passageway in front of me. Cresting a hill, I see a doe with two fawns playing in the road down at the bottom of the long grade ahead. The deer don't see me as much of a threat when I stop at the top of the hill to watch them. They're oblivious to flags and stripes and bars, just looking to enjoy the beautiful fall day.

Making my way up through Carthage and along the Carthage Pike, I'm surprised at the significant Quaker presence. After seeing all the Confederate flags this morning, now intermixed with the Friends gathering places the Quakers used, I recognize that I'm probably riding right along a seam of political dissonance that goes back a couple of hundred years. There are militant folks longing for a return to the days of slavery, glorifying the American Civil War with their Confederate flags, right alongside folks who won't fight in wars at all, and were among the most strident abolitionists in the days of the Civil War.

I find the National Road again in Knightstown, where I hope to find a good lunch diner. Spotting the Knightstown Diner, I ride over and dismount. Leaning my bike up against a post out front, looking around town to be sure this is the place I want to have lunch, a fella named Kevin walks past and kicks up a conversation with me.

"Where are you riding your bike from and to?" he asks.

"Well, ultimately from coast to coast, but today I started the other side of Indy, and will be finishing in Richmond."

"Very nice." He's not shocked at the distance, and I wonder if it might be somewhat common for cross-country cyclists to travel along the Old National Road through Knightstown. He continues with a cadence that feels like we're friends who just bumped into each other out here in front of the diner. "You stopping here for lunch?"

"I was thinking about it. Do you know this diner? Is it pretty good?"

"It's great—you'll really enjoy it." He smiles as he holds the door open for me. As I pass by, he says in a quiet voice, "Full disclosure, I own the place." I round to look at him, and his smile grows broad, then he swings past me and begins to introduce me to folks in the café.

One of the first people he pulls me toward is a woman sitting at the big table in front, then he heads toward the back of the diner after introducing us to one another. Turns out the woman coordinates the local Red Hat ladies, and we're just getting into a nice conversation when Kevin returns with additional folks he wants me to meet.

I feel like a celebrity as Kevin introduces me around, and eventually sits me down at a table right next to Bill and Curt, a couple of brothers about my age. Bill and Curt are from Kansas, not far from where I'm originally from in Kansas.

"So, you like cheeseburgers, right?" Bill asks as I start to open the menu.

"Sure, I like cheeseburgers."

Curt grabs the menu from me and folds it back up, turning toward the lunch counter and hollering to Kevin. "He wants the cheeseburger special, Kevin. Put some jalapeños on it." Turning to me, he adds, "You like jalapeños, right?"

I nod and shrug, clearly not in control of my lunch order.

"So tell me," Bill asks, "where you ridin' from and to?"

So I tell a short version of the story, at the end of which my cheeseburger arrives, along with a strawberry milkshake, which I didn't order.

"The milkshake is on the house," Kevin says. "It's Curt's favorite and since he was ordering for you I figured you'd probably like it too." He turns and walks away after delivering an admonishing look to Curt, who shrugs his shoulders and returns a look of innocent surprise at the rebuke.

While I dig in to my lunch, Bill and Curt fall into an easy narrative, filling in the gaps for each other, telling me their life stories. Just as I finish the cheeseburger, Kevin drops off a big plate of onion rings for us to share. Bill and Curt both acknowledge the plate with a nod and a smile, reaching for a ring, never breaking stride in their narrative. I look back and forth between Kevin as he walks away and the brothers as they continue telling me their story, wondering what prompted the order.

Curt sees the question on my face, and answers. "Oh, he just knows we like onion rings." Then he launches back into the narrative. I'm pretty sure that didn't actually answer my question . . .

I'm a little culture shocked as I take the onion ring that Bill offers. Bill and Curt are telling me pretty intimate details of their life stories, and while I appreciate that they confide in me, I'm also wondering why. I haven't initiated this level of sharing; I've pretty much just nodded and grunted agreement around bits of cheeseburger, fries, and onion rings as they've shared.

But then I remember the depth of the conversations I had with Ann back in Greencastle yesterday and Jeannette back in Missouri a week ago. Is this an instinctive human response to a traveler who comes into our camp? Sharing food and stories, drawing the traveler deeply into our lives for the brief moment they're with us? The Knightstown Diner belongs to these people. This is their place. They've invited me into their tribal place—a traveling vagabond invited into their circle for lunch.

While we've been eating and talking, the Red Hat ladies have been gathering at the big table at the front of the diner. The Red Hat Society is a thing that happens in small towns, or at least that's where I've noticed it or known of it. My experience has been that their gatherings are primarily social events that celebrate wisdom and fun, not necessarily in that order.

It's their meeting day, and they're raucous and joyous as they gather and chat. One of them, the one I met when I came in, calls me over and pulls me into their conversation. She introduces me around the table, telling me little bits about each of the ladies. One gal—who must have been over 80—just had liver surgery a couple of weeks ago. Here she was out and about, chatting it up with her Red Hat friends, just two weeks after a big surgery at 80-something years old.

I'll have some of what she's having . . .

I love the Red Hat ladies—both the concept in general and this group in particular. I love to feel our culture when it moves toward more respect for the wisdom and gifts that age can bring. The Red Hatters help us see that wisdom, and nudge us along.

Wabi-sabi.

A fella about my age walks in the front door, and the Red Hatters introduce me to him as well. Turns out he's the husband of one of the Red Hatters, and he comes to their meetings and plays piano now and again. After a brief chat, he wanders over to the old upright piano in the corner and starts to hammer out a little ragtime. I go back over to where Bill and Curt are sitting, and thank them for the conversation, then I walk up to the lunch counter and pay my check. Kevin is busy putting orders together but waves as I head toward the front door.

Several of the Red Hatters give me hugs as I go, and Bill holds the door for me as I walk out to where Curt waits for us. We jaw just a little while longer before saying our good-byes standing out on the sidewalk. The sound of muted ragtime drifts through the front window of the diner, birds squabble around us in the trees, a car slowly drifts past on the road now and then.

Here I am, in the middle of nowhere America, taking my leave from a wonderful tribe of folks who've just shared their place with me. A vagabond, sojourning down the highway, blessed by the goodwill and caring spirit of a tribe along the way.

A nice tailwind pushes me the final 40 miles of the day along the old national highway. Thoughts of ragtime, red hats, and generous spirits crowd into my memory as I pedal.

FINDING DAVE, AGAIN

Never go on trips with anyone you do not love.

Ernest Hemingway

My day ends in Richmond, where Dave arrives less than an hour after I do. We've touched base on the phone a couple of times during the day as he's covered the 1100 miles from Colorado and I've covered the 90 miles from Indy, preambling our way toward connecting at the end of the day. After dropping his rental car off and packing his gear onto his bike, he rides the couple of miles over to the Knights Inn where we've agreed to meet.

Dave and I fall immediately and without discussion into our tried and true traveling routine—showering, washing clothes in the sink, getting ready for supper. Routine feels good. Like home. A cat stretched out on a sunny window ledge. The smell of a kitchen you've known your whole life. A bend along a creek where you fished as a little boy.

I'm seeing the friendship between Dave and me in a different light this evening, likely a result of my last couple of days reflecting on relationships and the glue that holds people together. Dave and I are like a little tribe, with significant investment in the friendship we've developed. There's something about a friendship like this that transcends everything else. Time, place, circumstance—they all just fall to the side as we claim and feed the equity that is our friendship.

Laying on my bed, exchanging small talk with Dave as he sits on the edge of his bed watching the forecast on The Weather Channel, I realize that our friendship might also be one of the best reflections I can imagine of the notion of wabi-sabi. A friendship aged and proven, simple and strong, understated and deep. Steeped in a wisdom that expands and evolves with each great conversation we share.

There's another side to the notion of wabi-sabi that I recognize creeping around the edges of my consciousness this evening. It's a side that acknowledges imperfection and impermanence as deft components within the art of nature. Beauty in the transience of existence, beauty exposed only in the appreciation of the artful profundity of the aging impermanence of things.

I think back to my conversations with Cathy and Ann over the past couple of days, and on my reflections on my failures at relationships. I suppose a relationship isn't much different from any other living thing. Some plants are annuals, exploding with color and show, madly spreading seeds from which future plants can sprout, then dying after only one season. Other plants are perennial, returning each year from roots that survive the winter. Still others are woody plants that survive year after year above ground, weathering each winter in progression, slowly putting on solid growth in the spring, storing nutrients each summer to prepare for the following winter.

Each relationship we have as we travel our path is different. If we're really lucky, we'll have a few in this life that grow into solid oaks, showing weather and age, but thriving, surviving, and improving *because of* not *in spite of* age and adversity. I was blessed with a 30-year marriage that thrived and grew before withering. While there's sadness in this that those little gremlins will always be happy to remind me of, there's also great goodness that I should remember and be grateful for.

In the other bed, Dave reaches over and clicks off the lamp on the table beside him. I lay awake, watching lights from outside the partially closed curtain playing across the ceiling. I'm a lucky man to have the solid oak planking of a friendship with Dave in my life. I'm a lucky man to have been part of a marriage that lasted 30 years. I hope to be wise enough to recognize and appreciate the wise and imperfect people I will cross paths with as I continue down this road I'm on.

WAFFLE HOUSE

*The individual has always had to struggle to keep from
being overwhelmed by the tribe. If you try it, you will be
lonely often, and sometimes frightened. But no price is
too high to pay for the privilege of owning yourself.*

Attributed to **Friedrich Nietzsche**

DAY 32 • RICHMOND, INDIANA TO COLUMBUS, OHIO

A low foggy mist hangs over town as we pedal east out of
Richmond along the Old National Road. I cross another state
line here just after leaving Richmond. Ohio is my fifth state
on this eastern half of my journey, after spending the last four
days crossing first Illinois then Indiana.

A few miles out of town, the fog lifts her skirts and we're
treated to a rich and lustrous sunrise over the fields of western Ohio. In air thick with moisture, I pull over at the top of
a little rise to gaze across the scene. A farm down in the valley reaches up through the light mist that lays across the field,
a rich orange red glow from the morning sky pouring down
onto the scene.

A sailor might take warning at this red morning sky. In the back of my mind I know it could foretell the rainy day the weather forecasters are predicting. In my heart and soul, though, this spectacular pageant is a precious glimpse into the universe unfolding itself for me to enjoy.

Every day the sun rises, often in this sort of spectacle. If the sunrise isn't particularly wonderful, then perhaps it's the sunset. If not the sunset, then maybe some other magical nugget the world is sharing. Soaked in the richness of the morning, I realize that beauty like this only feels rare to me because I allow my life to keep me focused on the little details in front of me every day. I get up, have my breakfast, commute to work, give myself to the daily demands there . . .

If I were out in the world every morning, exposing myself to the elements along the road, feeling the chilly fog wet on my cheek, allowing myself to be open to the magic of the day, then I'd probably see more enchantment as the universe pours it over me every day. This isn't a new revelation, but standing off to the side of the road, captivated by the brilliance blooming in front of me, brings stark and singular clarity to the point.

To the drivers in the cars headed east, the sunrise is a bright nuisance in their eyes. The cars driving west are concentrating on the road ahead and not able to enjoy to the blossom behind them. I'm wrapped in my own bubble, able to experience this gift like no one else on the road. Well, there's Dave too, waiting up the road a bit for me.

As I ride up to him, he has a big smile on his face while he puts his camera away. "Pretty amazing sunrise," I say to him.

"'Amazing' barely covers it. Was the view better from back up on the rise?"

"Spectacular," I respond. I watch as he gazes back up to the top of the rise, apparently wrestling with whether or not he wants to ride back up the road a few hundred yards. "I took a lot of pictures." I throw this last bit out in case it helps him decide. In the end, he shrugs his shoulder with a decision to keep moving forward.

"It'd probably change by the time I got back up there anyway."

"Man, this kind of spectacle makes the mist bearable, doesn't it?"

"Indeed it does."

"Ready for some more pedaling?"

We head up the road, enjoying the evolving sunrise as we ride. This is a new and different Dave, or at least a version of Dave I don't get to see often. I've always known Dave to appreciate the roses along the side of the road, but not to spend too much time lollygagging in them. The little sunrise episode seemed an awful lot like lollygagging to me. I get the sense that Dave would have spent even more time enjoying the sunrise, and it felt odd being the one to suggest we get going.

Within about 10 miles we're able to drop down off the busier road onto a secondary road that's wonderful riding. This old secondary road may very well be the *Old Old National Road,* hinted at by an old covered bridge sitting by itself in a city park in the town of Lewisburg. I ride over to and around the bridge, a feeling of disappointment hanging over me. The bridge is clearly out of place here in the dry park, like a once-proud lion panting on the concrete in a cage at the zoo.

Why does this bother me, seeing the bridge like this? Isn't this a form of respect for the old bridge and the culture that created it? That's not how it feels, though. An old bridge, deconstructed, moved, and rebuilt in a place where it doesn't belong. It feels displayed, not respected. We've transformed it from a wonder to a spectacle. It's not really a covered bridge anymore, but a replica of what a bridge once was, yanked from its true place down in the moist woods across the creek to a dry and dusty park.

I suppose everything has a *true place* in the world. Maybe things can have many *true places,* some more true than others. If we move a thing from its true place into a museum, is it really the thing it once was any longer? Back in eastern Colorado and western Kansas, the land spoke of ancient people who were part of that place and the place was part of them. In Alton, I caught myself smiling at the notion of finding *my place* as I explored the nooks and attics of the old Butler's Quarters.

I think of old folks I know and have known in my life. What is it that makes some of them seem like they're past the crest of the hill and just coasting to the end, while some of them seem to be flying toward the crest right up to the very end? Could it be the same as the bridge in the park—that those over the crest have been moved out of the place or places where they're supposed to be in life, and end up feeling like a relic in a park?

Somewhere behind me is the midpoint of my life. I'm not sure how far back there it is, but there's no doubt there are more years behind me now than in front of me. I hope I can find ways to stay in *my places* and continue to climb to the very end.

Back on the road, I catch up with Dave. Waiting. We're back to our normal mode now—Dave waiting on Neil as Neil meanders through the roses. As always, he's nice about it and makes me feel like it's no problem at all. But I know better. The bit now feels too tight this morning to Dave, and he's chomping at it. It's Day One for him, and he's ready to get out and stretch his legs, to get some miles behind us.

The Waffle House in Brookville is friendlier than most, and this says a lot. Waffle Houses in general make customers feel welcome. There's a Waffle House close to where my brother lives in Kansas, and he goes there many mornings for breakfast. While the food is fine, I suspect he goes back there because they all smile and call out "Mornin' Erik" to him when he walks into the door. Sometimes when I go there, they'll remember me as well.

"Hey, it's Erik's brother," one of the gals will call out. Another one will look up, smile, and add, "Mornin' Erik's brother." To which I'll smile back, delighted to be there, feeling like I belong. That's why we like a place, isn't it? We feel like we belong. We feel like it's one of *our places,* like we're around *our people.*

A large contingent of Amish folks are enjoying breakfast at the Waffle House this morning. A couple of big vans are parked out in the parking lot, a dozen or so women and children in Amish dress are inside the Waffle House, and a handful of Amish men are outside gathered around a little structure in the park next door. The men gesticulate in animated conversation with one another, apparently engrossed in discussion revolving around the construction of the little structure. They laugh and nod now and then, enjoying the equity of their people, able to find a little spot to claim as their place.

As long as we have our people, we can carve out a place. I suppose it's always been like that, and this is the advantage we've gained in becoming so tribal. This congregation of Amish folks appears to be pretty tight-knit, and could probably establish a place nearly anywhere, so long as they have one another. They're likely here in town for a brief visit or chore, and they've forged *a place that's theirs* from the Waffle House and the park next to it. They're comfortable, enjoying this temporary bubble of place-ness that blooms wherever they are.

Dave and I finish our breakfast, and go find our place in the saddle. Truly, it does feel like my place. In the saddle, turning the pedals, headed down the road with Dave. Our own little bubble of place, nourished by the equity of our friendship.

I like my place. I like my people. I'm glad to be riding with Dave again.

BICYCLE BILL

Wisdom is oft-times nearer when we stoop
Than when we soar.

William Wordsworth, *The Excursion,* 1814

We make our way a little south, riding through downtown Dayton. While this adds a few miles to our day, it also lets us stay on bike paths for most of the day. I get us a little lost going through Dayton, but we find our way back to the Creekside Trail, which we follow into Xenia. At Xenia, we pick up the Ohio to Erie Trail, which will take us most of the way to Columbus.

I lived in Cincinnati for 12 years earlier in life, and today the weather is just like I remember countless days during those years—overcast and gray. The temperature is perfect for riding, though, and a little tailwind caresses my back as we fly along the trail.

The paved trail is flawless, making for a smooth and wonderful ride despite the damp and gray day around us. Farmland opens up on either side of us, mixed with deciduous forest now and then. As we clock along at a rapid clip, I recognize the harmony in my body and soul that I so often feel when I fall into a steady rhythm that blends hard work with miles ticking along beneath my wheels.

Life is good.

In London (yes we're still in Ohio), we stop to fill water bottles and take in a few calories. Leaning up against the side of the building, drinking water and eating something terribly unhealthy but wonderfully delicious, we watch an old fella riding his bike along the highway through town. His straggly gray hair is streaked with white, flying in the wind, a bushy beard pressed back against his weathered face.

"Hmmmm," I observe. "Hopefully we don't look quite that ragged as we make our way down the road."

Dave chuckles. "I was thinking about growing my hair and beard out. Maybe it's not such a good idea."

In the middle of our good-natured fun, we notice that the old fella has turned his bike around, and is riding up to the convenience store. Stopping right in front of us, he greets us as if we're best friends.

"So where you guys headed today?"

Dave and I look at each other, and Dave answers. "Started the day on the edge of Indiana, headed to Columbus today."

"Riding across the country?"

Dave and I both smile, Dave answers again, "Yeah," then a pause followed by a tone that makes you think you've said something really insightful, "We *are* riding across the country. What makes you think that?"

I love it when Dave uses that tone when he talks to me—makes me feel really smart. Our new friend obviously feels a little buoyed by the tone as well, and smiles a wise smile as he answers. "Just a feelin' I guess—the bags on the back of your bikes make it obvious that you're doing more than a day ride." After a pause where Dave and I are nodding, he adds, "Hey, I'm Bill. People just call me Bicycle Bill." He sticks out his hand, and we introduce ourselves as we shake hands.

"So you live here in town?" I ask.

"Yep. Livin' it up in London is what I always tell folks. It's not as expensive as most folks think!"

His subtle humor has me warming to him. Obviously a smarter guy than the impression that his wild look creates. I chuckle a bit, then he continues. "So where you guys from?"

We answer, and our conversation quickly turns to our route today. He tells us that we can get back on a bike trail that will take us most of the rest of the way to Columbus, and he offers to show us the way to the trailhead, since it's hard to find. As we meander through town, he chats amiably with us when he's not greeting the folks we ride past; nearly everyone is on a first-name basis with Bicycle Bill.

Bicycle Bill is clearly a fixture in town, and not in the pejorative way that my first impression led me to assume. Sometimes first impressions are a problem. My first glance at Bill dropped me immediately into presumptions that included homelessness and more. On the surface I saw a guy who was wild, scruffy, unkempt, maybe even a sandwich or two shy of a picnic. When he first approached us, I expected he'd be asking for a handout.

But in the ten minutes we spent together in the convenience store parking lot, the picture in my head started to change a bit, and I began seeing him as a pretty average guy who was probably as normal as Dave and me. (I grant you, that's not a particularly high bar to clear, but I'm just tryin' to make a point here.)

In the subsequent five minutes of riding together through town, it becomes clear to me that Bill is a respected member of this small-town community. A respected member whom some folks might even view as something akin to a wise elder.

How many golden opportunities do we miss in life because we misjudge the cover of a book? As a parent, I really worked on helping my kids understand the importance of the cover. "While it might not be fair," I'd say, "it's the way humans work in the world, so don't handicap yourself with a poor cover." Nothing fair about it. It's just the way of it.

Meandering through London, Ohio with Bicycle Bill, I'm realizing that unknowingly, I've failed to use this cultural knowledge to my advantage on the other side of the equation. I let myself judge covers too quickly and move on, and while this might be no big deal in many situations, how many opportunities do I miss to meet good folks like Bicycle Bill as a result?

We're built to make snap judgments. It's a big part of how we can process so much information and move through the world with such intelligence. We build patterns and buckets in our brains that let us quickly manage incoming information. Our senses are bombarded by incoming information all day long, and our minds are outstanding at taking the incoming information and sorting it into the patterns we've pre-built, dumping it into the right bucket so we can focus on the new information we're filtering.

It's the way we work. But I need to get better at consciously stepping out of the bucket brigade more often, at questioning whether or not things really fit into the buckets and patterns that I've built.

Bill drops us at the trailhead, and we make our way a few more miles on nice rail trail. When the trail ends on the west side of Columbus, we pick our way through the roads across the south side of town before finally reaching our destination on the southeast side of Columbus. Our route takes us along roads where a good portion of the drivers fall somewhere between rude and criminally negligent. We're repeatedly honked at by cars as they pass far too close, or cut off in ways that force us to slam on our brakes.

Having just spent time reflecting on the dangers of snap judgments based on sparse information, I find myself resisting the urge to classify Columbus, Ohio as one of the most unfriendly cities we've ridden through. But it's tough. Really, some of these drivers should be ashamed. I imagine a television show that chronicles their behavior, and broadcasts it once a week for the world to see. Kind of like the publishing of the names and addresses of sex offenders.

We need to be more public with our derision of conduct that's dangerous to our culture and our civilization. The driver of a car is in complete control of a machine weighing thousands of pounds, capable of inflicting instant death or injury to many people. Irresponsible behavior needs to be scorned publicly, and criminal actions should be punished criminally. MADD was so effective at getting tough laws passed for drunk driving; I'd love to see them campaign for punishment of other disdainful practices behind the wheel. Let's start with texting while driving, and see where we can go from there.

The first 100 miles of the day were a real cycling treat along beautiful Ohio cycling paths, and these final 20 miles show an ugly side of people that I'd like to put behind me. I'm looking forward to seeing the happier, healthier, wonderful side of people that's so much more fun to be around.

We find the Comfort Inn southeast of Columbus, eat some fast food, and settle into a rowdy night on our floor since we're surrounded by families here for a softball tournament, families who feel that it's okay to party up and down the hallways until 3:00 in the morning. Certainly a happier side of people, and in happiness there is health, after all. And I'm sure they feel wonderful.

But I'm not feeling quite so much of the happy thing. I suppose the smart thing to do would be to join them, have a few beers, and experience the wonderfulness with them. But with 131 miles to ride tomorrow, I find myself wrapping extra pillows around my head, trying desperately to discover just a little sleep.

THE EAST

I have found out there ain't no surer
way to find out whether you like people
or hate them than to travel with them.

Mark Twain, *Tom Sawyer Abroad*

EQUINOX

Travel is fatal to prejudice, bigotry, and narrow-mindedness, and many of our people need it sorely on these accounts. Broad, wholesome, charitable views of men and things cannot be acquired by vegetating in one little corner of the earth all one's lifetime.

Mark Twain, *The Innocents Abroad*

DAY 33 • COLUMBUS TO ST. CLAIRSVILLE, OHIO (AUTUMNAL EQUINOX)

Next morning rise and shine is accompanied by some grousing on my part about loud partying late at night. Since the families around me set the precedent that sharing fun and joy in noisy rooms and hallways is okay, I'm more than happy to share some of my 5:30 a.m. happiness.

"Oh wait, I think I forgot something," I exclaim to Dave as we roll our bikes out of the room. Oops, the door just accidentally slammed, probably a little too loudly.

Dave smiles, but doesn't answer. Dave's nicer than I am. I can be a jerk about this sort of thing. Of course, Dave is better at sleeping through noise than I am, and my inability to sleep through all the noise last night is certainly deteriorating my capacity for niceness this morning. A short minute later— probably just enough time for someone to drift back to sleep— I discover the missing whatever-it-was that I forgot, and exit the room for a second time. Darn, the door slammed again . . .

"Found it!" I exclaim loudly to Dave, who's meandered up to the far end of the hall where he's holding the elevator door for me. He's a saint for putting up with me. I can be so embarrassing sometimes.

It's about 200% humidity outside the hotel as we saddle up. My crankiness over lack of sleep is quickly replaced by the euphoria I always feel early in the morning as we glide through the predawn twilight, breathing in the moist air, enjoying streets that are mostly empty as we meander east and north through the suburbs of Columbus.

We make our way back up to the Old National Road as it parallels I-70. It's a four-lane highway that's essentially deserted of cars. I realize it's a Saturday morning, which could account for the low traffic volume, but it looks like a highway that doesn't see much use. After a few miles, the road narrows back down to two lanes and begins to feel very much like the Old National Pike.

It strikes me that right here, this morning, the road around me has shifted in historical time. It was the early 1800s when this old pike was commissioned by a young nation, and the remnants and architecture dating back that far is becoming evident along the side of the road. Back then, this was considered *western wilderness,* being tamed by this new road reaching out and offering a path for commerce and expansion. This morning, riding my bike along the pleasant old road, up and down the increasing hills, I've entered what is today considered *the East.*

Somewhere back in Kansas, things shifted for me as well. It felt like I left *the West* and entered *the Midwest.* From eastern Kansas to central Ohio, things have felt very much like *the Midwest* to me. Now, entering the hilly terrain of eastern Ohio, seeing the old history from the early 1800s, it feels like I'm crossing into something like *the East.*

Today is the Autumnal Equinox. I'm sure there are folks out in the world doing things that news networks are reporting on, things of great import, but in my little world, the two biggest stories of the morning are my realization that it's the Autumnal Equinox, and my observation that we've transitioned into something that feels like the East.

This delights me in a couple of ways. The first is my appreciation of how much I enjoy my place in the world when I'm cut off from the mass media and instant news of modern civilization. I've felt this often in life, when I've had extended time "in the wilderness" in one way or another. I always marvel at it. I'm so much more connected to the moment when I dispel myself of the myth that today's headlines are more important than the little slice of wonder that the universe has given to me, right here and right now.

The other thing I'm appreciating as I glide along the deserted highway is the idea of the equinox. A point of change. A turning. The autumnal equinox, in particular, is that time when we celebrate the harvest. We look back with thanks, and look forward with hope. The Jewish New Year always falls at this time of year, though it's not tied to the equinox. Still, today we sit in that ten-day period between Rosh Hashanah and Yom Kippur, coming up to the holiest of days next week. It's a time of atonement for mistakes made, a time to forgive and be forgiven. Most important, a time for looking forward.

I smile at the synchronicity of the little moment the universe is sharing with me. It's a time to let go of regret for things not said or not done, and remorse for things said or done. A time to forgive and be forgiven. Looking up the deserted road in front of me, seeing the history lining this old pike, I'm thankful to be on this road that leads into the future, lined with some structure from the past.

We hit Zanesville at about 60 miles for the day, and stop for lunch at Juanita's Restaurant. It's a small local dive—my kind of place. The food in these sorts of diners is a real crapshoot—sometimes you end up with really great food, and sometimes you end up with really not-so-great food. But culinary adventure is fun, and besides, the ambiance is the real reason I can't stay away from these jewels.

Turns out the food at Juanita's is pretty decent, and the ambiance is more than worth the risk of adventure, as we discover a great deal of local gossip by eavesdropping on several colorful conversations. By the time we leave, our bellies are full of decent food and our imaginations are overflowing with local color.

Just after leaving Juanita's, we cross the historic Y-Bridge in Zanesville, and weave our way through town. Old limestone buildings are well-maintained on either side of the road as we meander and gander our way along the streets of this grand old town dressed for bygone times.

Just after Cambridge, US 40 is swallowed up by I-70. As a result, in Cambridge we're forced to leave US 40 and angle our way southeast on some state highways, then angle back northeast to rejoin US 40 around St. Clairsville. When planning the trip, I struggled with this little stretch, wishing we could just stay on the interstate for this section; bicycles aren't allows on the interstate highways in Ohio.

Turns out these are some of the prettiest roads of the trip so far. Gentle rolling hills, low traffic volume, and courteous drivers. As a bonus, we find a little rail trail running beside the road for a few miles just as we leave Cambridge. In the little town of Salesville, we get turned around and end up on a side street, where we're warmly greeted by a young woman unloading groceries.

In more populated areas, it's unlikely that a young woman would warmly greet and strike up a conversation with a couple of guys on bicycles outside her home as she unloads groceries. I'm not making any judgments of right or wrong, I'm just observing something about our cultural guidelines and the way things work in our society. But here in tiny little Salesville, in rural Ohio, this gal is genuinely and innocently interested in who we are, where we're from, and where we're going.

One of the regrets I'll have on this trip is that I don't stop and chat with her. We exchange a few friendly words with each other, but I can tell she'd really like it if we stopped and visited for a bit.

Back to the regrets thing, right? I think this gal was just looking for a little conversation from the larger world. Maybe she was a fellow cyclist curious about our route. Maybe she was bored, looking for a few words about adventure. Whatever it was, I'm guessing that stopping and chatting on the curb outside her house would have brought some joy into her life, and probably enriched my life as well. Instead, it's a regret for a thing not done.

After making our way back to the Old National Road west of St. Clairsville, I'm feeling a bit pressed and pressured by the change in the traffic around me. Folks on the road feel more intent on getting somewhere, and on making good time. There's nothing carefree or relaxed about the way people are driving. It's Saturday, so there's no *rush hour* factor to consider. It's just the transition off of the nice backroads we've been experiencing for the last few hours and back to a more primary thoroughfare.

Nobody along the back roads has any big point *A* or point *B* they're moving from or to, and you pick that up from the drivers as they pass, from the stops along the way. It's all local traffic—folks going to a neighbor's, or to the grocery, or to complete a chore. Mom bringing lunch to Dad out in the field as he rakes that last cutting of hay for the season.

Folks along the back roads are living right here, in this little piece of the universe. You feel that in the world as you pedal through it. You feel them sharing their slice of the universe with you. They're hosting you on the road that winds its way through their lives. There are more smiles, more waves.

More moms with groceries in their arms wondering where you've been and where you're going.

I think this must be what we felt back in the middle of the country, so welcome and safe as we rode across Kansas along US 160. Nobody was using that highway to get from *A* to *B*. There were too many other options for moving west to east. Folks along that road lived there, and we were guests in their home as we rode.

Here, back on US 40, I feel the difference. This is still a road that's more *local* than the interstate, but folks along this road feel more intent on getting someplace. More interested in being somewhere else. Less content with the place they are in the universe at this moment.

Having picked up a tiny bit of tailwind, we fly along the road at a pretty good clip. I'm out in front of Dave, which is a change. Part of me wonders if this is one of those rare times when I'm a little stronger than Dave, but most of me is pretty sure he's just letting me ride out front for a change. Either way, it feels good to be in front, and I'm reminded again of that psychological boost we get when we get to be out front, leading the charge.

THE ANATOMY OF A BAD DECISION

*Ah how shameless—the way these mortals blame the gods.
From us alone they say come all their miseries yes but they
themselves with their own reckless ways compound their
pains beyond their proper share.*

Homer, *The Odyssey*

Like Zanesville, St. Clairsville is a charming old town from the early part of the nineteenth century. Old limestone buildings, well built and well cared for, line the road through town. A thunderstorm behind us to the west chases us along the highway and through town, and we feel raindrops a few times as the front edge of the storm dances along our backs.

Our home for the night here is nice—one of the nights when we get to use Hilton points to stay. We've covered 130 miles today, and we ended the day feeling strong. Bolstered by the plentiful protein and high-quality calories in a big steak dinner, we realize that we're very close to completing this journey. Our good day of riding and good food mix to create a euphoria in both Dave and I, and we start to smell the barn at the end of the trail.

"You know," Dave says over dinner, "we've only got three days of riding and we're at the salt water on the right side of the continent."

"It doesn't feel like we're that close. But yeah, you're right. Tomorrow we end up at a B&B along the GAP trail, then a couple of easy days of riding and it's done."

We both cut another slice of steak, and I watch Dave's gaze fix on that point B that we're drawing very close to now. At every previous point along this ride, there would be a little tension here, a little push and pull, as Dave would want to move a little faster toward point B, and Neil would want to smell a few more roses. But tonight is different, and I find myself eager to explore options to pull ourselves more quickly to the finish line, a line that's starting to feel like a victory, or at the very least a big accomplishment.

I throw a little bait out there. "You know, I'm feelin' pretty good, and could skip the rest day. How are you feeling?"

"I was just thinking the same thing. I can easily skip the rest day and arrive a day earlier. Could we make the changes to the hotel reservations?"

"I bet we can. We'll get on the phone after supper and try."

When planning this trip, a persistent bit of advice I got from every single person I talked to in this part of the country was to avoid US 40 through western Pennsylvania and into Cumberland. The consistent message I got was that traffic is heavy, drivers are rude, and the hills are awful. So I planned the route to swing a little out of our way toward Pittsburgh, jump on the Great Allegheny Passage (GAP) trail, and ride this flat rail trail all the way to Cumberland.

Sitting here in front of a rich meal, we've agreed now to cutting our trip short a day by removing a rest day. Reasonable men would stop now, stick to the current route, drop the rest day, and arrive at our destination a day early. But something drives both of us tonight to look for ways to arrive at the finish line just a little more quickly. It's not reasonable.

This is unusual for me. My normal M.O. on the trip so far has been to detour into most any rose garden I can find to smell a few extra roses. While the GAP trail adds miles to the trip, it also takes us along a beautiful rail trail that I'd likely enjoy as much as I enjoyed the Katy Trail back in Missouri. I feel this change in my normal pattern, and wonder about it.

I checked email a little bit ago at the concierge desk, and found an email from Christine. Remember Christine? The girl from the tennis court back in college? From the magical summer day of falling in love in the hills of Kansas? We've continued our conversation since my initial contact with her about routes, and those conversations and emails have escalated. I don't have a good name for what the conversations have escalated into, but I imagine most of us can identify with it.

Some cocktail of emotions we experience when we feel good chemistry with someone and are driven toward finding where the chemistry leads. Irrational behavior that happens at the beginning stages of a relationship, when it feels like the connection wants to blossom and grow a little, like those tiny early leaves on a plant as it reaches for light that something deep inside its DNA knows is there.

Her email was short, sweet, and to the point. All she said was, "Hurry."

Hurry. How much of my judgment tonight is impaired by that word? I watch, feeling almost like a bystander, as two normally reasonable men plummet toward unreasonable decisions. Nothing good ever starts with two men sharing a beer, saying things like *watch this*.

Watch this.

The warmth of good beer bolsters our cockiness, suppressing objectivity and prudence, greasing the skids as we creep along the precipice of irrationality, preparing for our plunge into the abyss of dumb and dumber.

Dave starts the tumble by asking, "So, how many miles would it save us to just stay on US 40 and skip the GAP trail?"

"I can't remember for sure. Maybe 20 or 30?"

After a pause, Dave continues. "Really, the hills haven't been that bad. I've actually enjoyed them."

"I agree. Today was one of the prettiest days of riding we've seen across the whole country. Are you wondering if maybe we should just stay on US 40 all the way to Cumberland?"

"Well, yeah, I guess I am. What are your thoughts?"

"There were three big reasons for avoiding US 40: Traffic, lack of shoulder, and hills. Tomorrow is Sunday, so traffic should be low, reducing the impact of the first two factors. If we're okay with the hills, then really, I don't see any reason not to stay on the highway."

Well, other than the fact that this was the most adamant advice I got from every single person I talked to ahead of time—to avoid this section of US 40. But see how this goes? It's so easy for two relatively rational and intelligent men to talk themselves into really stupid things when they just had a great day of riding, which surely raises testosterone levels. Add a couple of beers, and stir the whole thing up with the unavoidable "mine's bigger than yours" thing that happens when a couple of guys start bantering back and forth, challenging each other in the most subtle and implicit ways.

"Right," Dave continues, "and we can avoid a day of riding on that crushed rock."

"Yeah, the riding on it isn't so bad, but the dust just gunks up the chain. And the hills haven't been bad at all. I can't imagine they'll change much tomorrow."

Notice the subtle bravado? *Me a man. Me not afraid of little hill. Me eat hills for lunch!*

We go to bed feeling particularly good, and sleep in the comfort of a fantasy that tomorrow we'll cruise down beautiful rolling highways much like today. As I lay in bed, I recognize that my contribution to our decision to shave our rest day out of the trip was guided *in part* by my eagerness to feel the achievement at the end of the ride.

I also recognize the pull of something else. Something both soft and urgent. Something that pulls me into the future while remembering a moment far in the past.

Hurry was all she said.

INTO THE ABYSS

There is no education like adversity.

Benjamin Disraeli, *Endymion*

DAY 34 • ST. CLAIRSVILLE, OHIO TO GRANTSVILLE, MARYLAND

A humid sunrise greets us in the morning, the moist air adding to the early morning chill as we fly down a steep drop from St. Clairsville and across Wheeling Creek. The road meanders along the flats beside the creek for a few miles, through old towns and past 200 years of history, a light mist rolling out from the creek and onto the road occasionally.

Dave and I walk our bikes across the historic suspension bridge in Wheeling and into West Virginia, soaking up the charm of the old river, breathing in the beauty of a clear and brisk early autumn Sunday morning as it blooms around us. This old bridge was built in the middle of the 19th century— the first bridge across the Ohio River—and spent two years as the longest suspension bridge in the world. A relic of engineering beauty that's only enjoyed by local folks these days.

In Wheeling, we begin to rely heavily on the maps I planned and loaded into my Garmin. Prior to this as we've

crossed the country, we've just used these maps as a backup—
something to get us back on track if we stray too far from our
planned route as we meander. Here in Wheeling, we take whatever turns the Garmin tells us to take, and are rewarded with
a wonderful ride through town, following an excellent bicycle
path for several miles along an old railroad grade, dropping
us off in Elm Grove east of Wheeling.

Another 15 miles or so down the road, just after entering
Pennsylvania, my Garmin tells me I'm off my route. I'm still
on US 40, but I just passed a turnoff to West Alexander. Dave
and I consult about this, and after our good experience earlier
in the day following my pre-mapped route in the Garmin, we
decide to trust the route I loaded into the Garmin, and follow
the older road. Who knows, maybe up ahead is another spot
where US 40 disappears into I-70 for a few miles.

This turns out to be a beautiful old road—probably the
Old Old National Pike. But it's eight or ten miles of slow and
rattly gravel road not suited for road bikes, and probably eats
up an extra hour of the day. Looking back on the route later,
I'll realize that I could have stayed on Route 40, and while
the old gravel route is pretty, we'll desperately want this hour
back later in the day.

In Washington we make our final decision to go with the
US 40 route rather than the GAP route. We're taking in a big
breakfast/lunch at the Bob Evans, about 40 miles into our day,
and the difficult riding and extra time we've spent this morning have knocked our cockiness back just a tiny bit. And yet,
we're still convinced we're smarter than all the people from
whom I sought route advice when planning our route. We're
still willing to launch ourselves down this next stretch of highway against all that helpful input from good people.

Arrogance and cockiness are so dangerous when mixed
with a little optimism and euphoria. Watch this? Don't try
this at home.

Later that night, an old fella will deliver pizza to our
room in Grantsville, Maryland. The pizza will taste like one

of the best things I've ever consumed. I'll soak my sore body in a hot shower, and update those closest to me that I'm safe and fine. Of course, they wouldn't have known to be worried—they would have had no idea that I just spent what Dave and I will look back on as our day from hell riding through western Pennsylvania.

Not that everything about the day or the ride is bad. We roll through beautiful countryside, with stunning scenery along rivers and down across valleys. Generally, I suspect the folks in the towns we ride through and in the cars that pass us are really nice, just like everywhere else. At least the ones who aren't throwing empty beer bottles at us, but I'm getting ahead of myself . . .

Let's talk about hills, and about climbing hills on a bike. Being from Colorado, I love to climb mountain roads on my bike. Few things are as satisfying as a nice five- or ten-mile climb, your body finding a delectable harmony of work, a rhythm of muscles and heart and lungs, climaxing with a summit from which you can see for miles. I like to stop for just a minute at the summit, enjoying the view while I consume calories that will soak into my body during the descent.

The descent. That wonderful reward for the hard work of climbing. Screaming downhill, bending into corners, wrapped in the wind. Delicious recompense.

These hills in western Pennsylvania are nothing at all like the mountains of Colorado. They're short and steep, with no time to enjoy either the going up or the coming down. The coming down lasts only seconds, and when I hit the bottom, the turn back up is so abrupt that I feel like I must have hit a runaway truck ramp. Momentum carries me about 23 inches up the other side before I'm pushing the cranks again.

When I start pushing the cranks, I've lost any rhythm I was developing on the last uphill section, and find myself standing up on the pedals trying to find a little shred of that climbing euphoria that's so nice to feel. The muscles in my legs ache with the constant on-again, off-again pressure I'm putting on them, and my heart is very confused by the whole thing, clearly rebelling against my fickle demands.

Occasionally a hill is long enough to allow me to start feeling a little comfortable sweet spot before I hit the top, falling into a comfortable rhythm of exertion. But then the summit of that particular hill comes, and the little eight-second ride to the bottom begins, and the whole little cycle of misery starts up again.

There's a ride we like to do in Colorado called the Triple Bypass. It's a route from the Denver area to a spot just west of Vail. Something close to 120 miles, with 11,000 or 12,000 feet of climbing in the day. It's a big-deal ride for those who can get into shape for it by July each year. All that elevation gain is spread out over three climbs. For the 10 or so hours of riding, you're essentially climbing or descending three long passes.

Today, we're in three states. We'll finish the day at just shy of 120 miles, with 11,400 feet of total elevation gain. That gain will happen in tiny little chunks—climb 200 feet, then descend 190 feet, then climb 200 feet, descend 190 feet. Over and over, with the tiniest of net gain on each climb. Misery doled out in tiny little sections, spread out over hours.

And these hills aren't gentle rollers. They're consistently 6% to 9% grade, with a grueling 12% section thrown in now and then for fun. That's steep enough to need brakes occasionally on the descent. So here we are, climbing the same 200 feet of elevation gain over and over, and just to throw some insult on top of the injury, we have to brake on the descent.

C'mon. Really?

Then there's the road. Clearly, bicycle traffic was not part of planning for this road. Often there's no shoulder at all, and when there is a small shoulder, it's generally full of glass and other crap that we want no part of.

It's Sunday, so I suspect the traffic is much lighter than it would be on a weekday. It's not that the traffic is light—I'm just looking for a bright spot here. Since we made such a bad judgment call, staying on US 40 when we could have ridden on the GAP trail, I want to believe we didn't have to endure as much traffic as we would have on a weekday. Again, just looking for a little tiny glimmer of something positive to say about these miles.

After a beautiful long descent into the town of Brownsville, we cross a wonderful old bridge, then find a shady place to rest and take in calories. A few miles back, Dave commented that at the rate we're going, we'll run out of either legs or light before we get to Grantsville. As always, Dave's been doing the constant calculations, and knows that we won't make our destination by dark unless our pace increases. The likelihood of our pace increasing is only slightly greater than zero, since our legs are clearly suffering.

Back down the road, when Dave said those words, I heard them as I took a picture of a beautiful old home along the road. My tiny little mind has Grantsville as our destination for the day, and just hasn't yet caught up to Dave's real and accurate prediction. I still have point *B* in my mind, and anything short of reaching point *B* just seems like a foreign language to me.

To hear Dave tell it, when he made that comment to me, I looked at him like he had two heads. From his perspective, I was saying, *"Heck, let's buck up man, we can do it."* The reality is that I just hadn't caught up with his reasonable logic yet.

I guess that's why we should always do these things with a good friend. It's pretty unlikely that two guys are both gonna have their brains engaged at any given time. Even if one of them uses sound logic to try to facilitate reasonable decision making, the other one is likely to be engaged in some sort of fantasy, or deluded by visions of unreasonable accomplishment, which will only make the reasonable one cast aside logic once he feels challenged by the foolish zeal of the other.

If not for this craziness, would the wheel ever have been invented? Would the Atlantic ever have been crossed? Would we ever have landed on the moon? Would Captain Smith ever have maintained his course with the Titanic in the face of iceberg warnings? Would Napoleon ever have failed so miserably in his invasion of Russia or his campaign at Waterloo?

Well, our day doesn't turn into Waterloo, but some shots might get fired, or someone might want to fire some.

BEER BOTTLES, GUNS, AND PIZZA

Whoever fights monsters should see to it that in the process he does not become a monster. And if you gaze long enough into an abyss, the abyss will gaze back into you.

Friedrich Nietzsche

Leaving Uniontown in Pennsylvania, we're treated to our one and only long climb of the day, and it feels pretty good. We climb for two or three miles, gaining 1300 feet, and while it's nothing like a Colorado climb, it's a whole lot more satisfying than what we've had all day. By the time we reach the top, I'm hopeful that maybe now the pointless up and down will stop for a while. The view from this summit is beautiful as we savor one of today's rare moments of optimism.

Climbing back into the saddle, I've just reached speed on the descent when I feel something crash against my back and hear the tinkling of glass shattering. Looking up, I see a red pickup truck speeding past me rolling the window up, and realize these yahoos just threw a beer bottle at me out of their truck window. And connected.

Luckily, they didn't hit me in the head, but across my lower back. Luckily, the bottle connected at an angle where it would break, rather than delivering all its force into my spine where something in me might break. Luckily, I don't have a gun handy.

Full disclosure: I own guns and like guns. However, I'm not a fan of folks carrying them around with them, and this incident is the perfect example of why I feel that way. Things can escalate too quickly, go too far, and end up in bad places.

In this moment, along this highway in Pennsylvania, I'm attacked by some idiot for no reason. Without a doubt, it's an attack that could easily kill me, either by hitting me in the head, breaking my spine, or causing me to crash into traffic around me. It's cowardice of the worse kind—attacking someone from behind and running away quickly so they don't get their hands on you. In any other circumstance, this would be considered assault with a deadly weapon, netting the perpetrator jail time.

Maybe his view of the world is so small that it doesn't include room for anyone who doesn't drive a red pickup truck like him. Maybe he's a sociopath. Maybe he's just really stupid. I have no idea why he did what he did. But if I could have gotten a gun into my hands quickly, I'm pretty sure I would have been sending lead into the back of his truck. Would it have been self-defense? Maybe. But somebody might have actually ended up hurt or dead. Maybe somebody innocent. How many lives might have changed as a result?

Dave and I talk it over on the side of the road. I'm clearly hopped up on adrenalin, and want some sort of retribution. But there's nothing to be done. We can call the cops and report it, but if this is like most places in the country, they don't take attacks on cyclists seriously. Plus, it'll just cost us precious daylight that we're losing very quickly.

I swallow my indignation and channel my adrenalin into pounding the pedals for a few miles down the road, hoping I'll see a red pickup truck stopped at a convenience store or someplace else in the next few miles. The guys in the truck are almost certainly cowards who'll cringe and weasel if confronted. Predictably, there's no red truck to be seen along the way, and in a couple of hours I'm gonna regret the extra energy I'm wasting as I vent my anger.

We're still several miles from Grantsville as we cross into Maryland and turn our lights on. I wear a Vis360 helmet light, which provides good visibility behind me, and also gives me a little light in front when it gets really dark. Dave has a very small light that shines forward, giving him a very small amount of light—really only enough light to be helpful if we're only riding a few miles an hour.

Dave is a better minimalist than I am. I think I'm pretty good at keeping my pack down to only the essentials, and my pack is certainly minuscule compared to those carried by most folks who tour on bicycles. But Dave takes the art of minimalism to a level that only a few modern humans are likely to achieve. While the pants I carry to change to in the evening after riding are very lightweight, they are long slacks. Dave carries a pair of running shorts that probably weigh 10 grams. The evening shirt I carry is also very lightweight, but the micro-thin t-shirt that Dave carries is probably half the weight.

Most of the time, I have to say I think Dave is the wiser of the two of us when it comes to this stuff. Generally, I could have gotten by just fine with running shorts and the light t-shirt. But in this case—in the case of how much illumination to carry —I highly recommend Neil's approach over Dave's.

I look back over my shoulder, and see Dave about 30 yards back. It's dark now. Not just twilight anymore, not just almost dark, but dark. The road in front of us is a black shape disappearing into the trees. I sense that Dave wants to stay behind me so he has a light to follow, as he's really unable to make out anything about the road. However, at the same time, I really want to be behind Dave so cars approaching from behind see my rear flashing light first.

I take Dave's lead on this, and stay in front of him to help him avoid running off the road or riding down the center of the road. It's late September, and we're up fairly high by eastern mountain standards. As soon as the sun dropped below the horizon, the temperature started to drop rapidly. If it were daylight, we could ride harder to try to generate heat, but we have to take it easy and slow in the darkness, exacerbating the effect of the cold. I'm wearing every layer I have, and I'm shivering.

We're in a rotten place. I'm picking my way down a descent, squeezing the brakes to avoid over-riding my meager headlight. Shivering violently, my exposed knees are aching with the cold. I hit the bottom of the hill and start to turn the cranks to climb the other side, when I'm treated to screaming pain in my knees. They've been working all day long, enduring the wear and tear that turning the cranks 50,000 times will generate, and now they're being iced-down in rapid fashion by 30-something degree air rushing across them in the descent.

When we hit the bottom and I ask them to start turning again, they endeavor to decline. Not so politely, I might add.

We go through this little routine a few times on the hills approaching Grantsville. Me coaxing my knees painfully back into a cranking routine at the bottom of each descent, them screaming their objections, us making our way ever so slowly up the other side. I always get them warmed back up so they'll endure a bit of pressure, but that usually happens about the time we hit the top of the climb and start the freezing descent again.

I'm at the bottom of a hill, going around a sharp little corner. Up the road are lights, so I assume we must be close to Grantsville. I try turning my knees, and they refuse. Really; they just say no. I have a moment of panic, realizing I'll need to unclip and stop riding here if I can't get some motion out of them, because we're about to start a little climb again.

Dave goes around me, frustrated I'm sure by these little episodes of nearly coming to a stop at the bottom of each hill, followed by the very slow progress up the side as Neil and his knees engage in a battle of wits, pain, and suffering. Here, at the bottom of this final hill, Neil appears to have lost the battle, and Dave is just too tired of the day to give a damn. Around me he goes, headed into the light on the road up ahead.

As rotten as we feel right now, it might as well have been that glorious light at the end of a near-death experience.

I eventually cajole my knees into turning for me again. We're not really that many clicks short of delirious in our suffering when I catch up with Dave, and we spot the Casselman Inn on our left. Few sights in the universe can compare with that of a warm inn at the end of a long day of suffering.

We make our way to our room and call the local pizza parlor to order delivery of the biggest pizza they make, covered in every form of meat they can find. Dave's still in the shower when our pizza debauchery arrives, and I don't wait for him before tearing into it like a hyena over a gazelle on the plains of Africa. I don't think I even wait for the door to close on the pizza delivery guy.

My Garmin tells me I burned 8400 calories today. To put that into perspective, I think the average male my age needs to try to take in something like 2000 calories a day to be healthy. Less than that and most of us will lose weight. Back in my "olden days," when I would backpack a lot, I would pack my food to give me 3000 to 3500 calories a day, which was the recommended intake for a very active male. I suppose it's possible to take in 8400 calories in a day, but it would involve a *lot* of eating.

Which helps to explain the whole *hyena over a gazelle on the plains of Africa* behavior, as well as the unnaturally good taste the pizza seems to have.

A long hot shower later, with a belly stuffed with meat and pizza, I drift off to sleep. I'm struck by the joy I feel at tiny comforts. This cheap little hotel room, smelling of pizza, with the heat turned way up, feels like a little slice of heaven.

Once again, it comes into focus. Our lives are so easy, comfortable, and consistent. We live in the middle of comfort, the lap of luxury by global standards. We're only able to appreciate the comfort and luxury that surrounds us each day if we allow ourselves to ride along the edge of discomfort for a while.

Gandhi's observation that some folks are so hungry that they can only see God in the form of bread comes to mind, reminding me again that hunger can sometimes help bring life into better focus. Darkness, indeed, helps us see the glory of light.

Hereafter, Dave and I will refer to this day as our *day from hell* on our trip across the nation. I suppose with all the heaven we've been treated to on this journey, a little taste of hell now and then isn't such a bad thing.

CROSSING THE EASTERN DIVIDE

The robbed that smiles, steals something from the thief.
William Shakespeare, *Othello*

DAY 35 • GRANTSVILLE TO HAGERSTOWN, MARYLAND

Crisp autumn air greets us again in the morning. Heaven has returned, and dawns around us as we roll out into a beautiful Appalachian morning. A night of deep and restful sleep has pushed the anguish of our *day from hell* back into dark corners of memory where ugly things live, and I'm absorbed in a sense of euphoria that I can't quite explain. My Garmin informs me that it's 39 degrees as we head east on *Old 40*, making our way toward a destination we can nearly taste now.

We stop to admire a beautiful old bridge a hundred yards off to our north as we're leaving town. Built nearly 200 years ago, it's the old Casselman Bridge, which carried the National Road across the Casselman River. Once again, *Old Old 40* . . . Maybe *Old Old Old 40*?

Leaning against cold steel girders on this old bridge that carries the most recent version of US 40 across the river, I admire the beauty of the older bridge resting against the hillside a couple of hundred yards away, where it carried the older version of the highway. The sun from my right and a little behind me kisses the eastern horizon, painting a gleaming luster of autumn brilliance across the hillside beyond the old bridge. Reds and yellows peek out of the rich green background, a reminder of the autumn season we've entered. The delightful sunrise display amplifies the elation I feel in every corner of my being.

Like yesterday, there are rollers this morning, but they seem enjoyable and insignificant compared to yesterday's. It could be that the rollers really are less significant that yesterday's, or it could be that I'm just feeling better this morning. Either way, bliss has enveloped me completely, and I'm enjoying every mile we ride.

After a dozen or so miles of nice rollers, we come to a wonderful four-mile descent into Frostburg. The way hills work with Dave and me is that Dave is usually faster going up, and I'm usually faster going down. (Dave's usually stronger than I am, and I weigh more, which is the reason for this order of things.) But not today. Today Dave flies down the descent, and I catch up to him soon after slowing as we come into town.

Dave smiles easily. I suppose it comes from his generally positive outlook on things, maybe from the sense of happiness that always seems to surround him. Most of the time, his smile says something like, *"Yeah, I'm a pretty happy guy,"* or *"Oh yeah, that's a kind of funny thing, and I get it."* But right now, coasting into Frostburg on this chilly September morning, Dave's ear to ear smile is screaming, *"Holy shit, did you see that? I just destroyed the speed limit as we bombed down that hill into town! WHAT A BLAST!!!"*

Life is just so darned good right now. A gorgeous and crisp autumn morning, the trees beginning to turn, I just flew down a long hill without a bunch of pesky turns, I'm with my buddy Dave . . . The only thing that might improve this moment would be finding a quintessential country diner—something from about 100 years ago, decorated with aging booths that have never been upgraded, a counter with stools that swivel, and chicken fried steak that hangs off the edge of a dinner plate.

Just as the thought fills my mind, I notice the Princess Restaurant on our right in the middle of Frostburg.

Perfect.

Really.

We dive into a heaping plate of unhealthy calories, delicious and satisfying in a way that only chicken fried steak smothered in sausage gravy can be, then climb back into the saddle for another 10 or 11 miles of heavenly descent into Cumberland. Now I know that yesterday I was ragging on US 40. I know I went on and on about the rotten little hills, short steep ups and downs all day long, the bad traffic, the bad shoulder, all of it. But coming down out of the mountains, riding through Frostburg, and coasting easily into Cumberland is a wonderful little slice of rapture that makes up for some little portion of the misery we found yesterday.

We're looking for a bike shop this morning as we drop into Cumberland. Dave struggled with some tuning problems on his bike yesterday (as if the hills and road weren't enough) and really wants to try to get those issues resolved. As we meander into the older part of town, I'm remembering that there's a bike shop down at the trailhead for the Chesapeake & Ohio (C&O) Canal Trail. I'm able to recall this because last spring, I joined Ann and Junior Cornell on a wonderful tour they lead of the C&O Canal Trail, beginning in Cumberland. They organize these tours out of Shepherd's Spring Outdoor Ministry Center over in Sharpsburg, Maryland.

As I'm pulling up, there stands Ann Cornell, waving toward the south as their autumn group of cyclists leaves, headed down the path on their first day of riding for the trip. Ann stands here and does this three or four times a year. Six months ago I was riding down the path away from her as she waved, and here I am riding up to her at this moment six months later, as I cycle across the country.

It seems like a pretty cool thing to me—the timing of it, the serendipity, and all that. I have to confess, though, that I don't think Ann remembers me from Adam. One man's moment of serendipity is another woman's wacky lunatic on a bicycle . . .

We spend about an hour at Cumberland Trail Connection. It's a great little bike shop run by a couple of guys who love bikes. It's pretty common that bike shops in a location like this are all about renting and selling cheap bikes to folks they assume don't appreciate a nice bicycle. That's not the case here at Cumberland Trail Connection, as these guys are into all things cycling, love the sport, and love the machines.

Tribalness. It's conspicuous in how Dave and I interact with these fellas running the bike store. When we're out on the road, we're not really connected to or involved with folks in the cars that are flying past us. We have a little connection now and then sitting at a diner, enjoying food in the company of other folks who are enjoying food. But here at the bike store, we're among close tribal members—fellow aficionados of cycling, cycling gear, and all other things cycling. They're enjoying our stories of the road, and we're appreciating their expert hands adding loving touches and adjustments to our bikes.

Leaving Cumberland Trail Connection, we meander east along Highway 144 as it parallels I-68. Highway 144 is most likely *Old 40,* and it crosses I-68 a couple of times, avoiding the straightened and flattened version of the road where all the cars go now. Sometimes our route is far above the new 40, sometimes well below.

At one of those points where we're far below the new 40 (or I-68), we're stopped along the road taking in a few calories, and I look down the slope a ways. I see an old road crossing an old bridge—almost certainly *Old Old 40.* Maybe even the original bridge built across this creek back at the beginning of the nation, 200 years ago. Above me is the newest and most current version of US 40, I'm on the old version of US 40, and below me I can see a yet older version of the highway.

I have no idea why I find this stuff so fascinating.

In Hancock, we jump onto the Western Maryland Rail Trail. The sun filtering through the canopy above lays a carpet of dappled light along our paved trail, adding another layer of magic to the ride. The path is largely deserted on this weekday afternoon, and we pass only a few folks out enjoying the early autumn beauty over the eight or ten miles we're able to enjoy this gem of a trail. It's a delightful afternoon bike ride for us, and I'm a bit disappointed when we move over to US 40 again near the end of the trail.

We have our first chain failure of the trip here, as Dave's snaps on a small hill. While I carry a little section of chain and a chain tool, Dave doesn't. This wouldn't be a problem if we had the same equipment, but Dave has a 9-speed chain, and I have a 10-speed chain. We do enough of a repair to get us the final 15 or 20 miles for the day, but Dave knows that the link we added isn't as strong as needed because of the bad fit, and he'll need to ride carefully as a result, avoiding any rapid accelerations that might break the weak link.

On its own, this incident wouldn't warrant a mention by me as I write this book. But it's a big deal to Dave, and his memory of it later will taint the day for him. In my mind, we were able to rig up a temporary repair, get it fixed the next day, and life is back to really really good again. In Dave's mind, his failure to bring the right gear has left a blemish on a beautiful day, and caused us to lose many hours the next day waiting for a bike shop to open.

Preparation. What's enough, and what's not enough? Where do you draw the line? While we couldn't have prepared for every little event that might come along, we did want to have the basics covered. In planning, I never even thought about the fact that we had different chain sizes, and we both figured that since I had a bit of chain and a chain tool, we'd be okay. And really, how often does a chain break?

There are many mechanical failures we're not prepared for. It will be easy later for Dave to beat himself up over failing to bring along the right chain pieces, just like it will be easy for me to beat myself up for not bringing along a chain whip so I could have repaired my drive-side spokes back in Missouri.

But stuff happens. We're not perfect. We did a good job of preparing for this ride, and we've been able to handle most of what has come up. It could always be better, but then again, it could always be worse.

Finishing up the repair, wiping the grease off my fingers as best I can in the grass along the side of the road, I feel myself going through the mental recalibration, redefining where we are and what we do next. Highest in my recalibration efforts is a recognition of the goodness of our current situation. A beautiful day, a wonderful ride, a good friend with whom to share the tribulation of a broken chain.

We mount up and head down the road, Dave riding carefully on his wounded chain. I can feel his anguish, and I wish I could take some of it away from him. He feels guilty, like he failed at preparing well enough. Every mile he spends feeling guilty keeps him from enjoying this delightful autumn day.

How much of life do we miss when we wallow in our regrets? How much wonder am I missing day to day when I sink into anguish for the stupid things I've done? What's the trick to learning to let go of our failings, and embrace the goodness of the moment we're in? It's simple to say, but not at all easy to do.

The early autumn day around me swallows me in splendor as I pedal along on good road with light traffic. At an age where I'm easing through a doorway into the autumn of my life, I realize that too much of me is consumed by disappointment at my failings, grief over sorrows I've been part of. I need to learn to pedal along, and give myself to the joy of this moment, not regrets for moments that aren't here. Every fragment of life I spend on wishing for a moment other than the one I'm in is a fragment of life I miss.

Pedal, breathe, smile, and enjoy.

YOUNG LIONS

Old men are twice children.

Greek proverb

DAY 36 • HAGERSTOWN TO ANNAPOLIS, MARYLAND

Our final day of riding begins about 11:00 with a shiny new chain on Dave's bike, after a long wait for the bike shop in Hagerstown to open. With 100 miles to cover today, we're pushing pretty hard to try to make up for those early morning hours of riding we missed.

Most days, by 11:00 in the morning we'd have most of the day's miles behind us. In fact, I think there was probably a day or two on our journey when we were done or close to done by this hour. Such a late start to the day, almost assuring that we have to finish the day in the dark, would normally have Dave and I both feeling pretty anxious and out-of-sorts.

But all I feel is euphoria. It's been building over the last day or two, and is in full bloom today.

Exhilaration.

Almost intoxication.

After riding 3400-plus miles over thirty-something days across the country, the end of the ride is just around the corner. I can just barely see the light at the end of the road coming into view. I can feel it deep inside me, almost smell it.

Two different (and competing) emotions play inside me as I turn the cranks. On the one hand, this has been the adventure of a lifetime, and I don't want it to end. Oh the places I've been, the things I've seen, the people I've met, the sensations I've smelled . . . I don't want this to end. I want to keep feeling like this tomorrow, and the next day.

On the other hand is this unexpected sense of accomplishment that's building inside me with each pedal stroke. The accomplishment needs a ribbon tied around it, a point of completion. I feel the edges of the ribbon fluttering in the breeze as I push my way through the moist eastern air, and I very much want to tie that knot.

It's clear to me that we're not likely to make Annapolis by nightfall, and after our experience a couple of days ago arriving after dark, this should worry me. But I find I don't even care. It'll be whatever it is, and we'll deal with it.

We'll make it. There's no doubt in my mind that at the end of the day, we will have completed our journey across the continent.

This feels really good. Unexpected for some reason, and really good.

The ride across Maryland is filled with easy and pleasant rollers. Some easy climbs and long gentle descents. Now and then we end up with a little traffic, but it's never terrible. The air is moist and rich with the scents of the changing landscape around us. We wander off course a couple of times, enjoying each distraction as it comes.

We've teased each other about the wind gods all the way across the country. Our west-to-east trajectory was designed to put the wind at our back most of the time, and while we did have a few days of nice tailwinds, we faced wind more than we ran with it. But today, the wind gods smile on us all day long; there's never so much as a whisper of wind as we crank our way along the highway.

We descend down the road through old Ellicott City, cross the bridge, and become confused when my Garmin seems to want me to turn into a little parking lot. We try a couple of different routes for a few hundred yards, but I can see on the Garmin that these routes take us in the wrong directions. So we go ahead and turn into the parking lot, and are rewarded with a happy Garmin when we find the entrance to a little bike path hidden at the back.

We look at each other and smile, accepting a higher level of confidence in the route I'd programmed into the Garmin. The path seems to be used primarily by walkers, and lasts only a few miles before dropping us again onto city streets. After several miles of blindly following the Garmin through city streets, I'm again beginning to think I might have made a mapping mistake as it takes me down to the end of a street and wants me to get up on a sidewalk. Dave and I look at each other, shrug, and start riding down the sidewalk. Within yards, the sidewalk opens up onto the Quad at the University of Maryland.

We slow to a walking pace for the short distance across the Quad, enjoying the scenery immensely. We swear undying allegiance to the Garmin, based on its kindness in dragging us through this beautiful setting late in the day. The treat is wonderful but short, and we're soon dropped onto university streets.

Riding along a combination of trails and streets, approaching a point where we'll jump onto the Baltimore and Annapolis Trail for the final miles, we find ourselves riding with a young fella who's in the Baltimore area on business. He matches our pace as we pass him, and we chat amiably for a mile or two as we ride together.

There's a funny little thing that happens with cyclists. Well okay, maybe not with all cyclists, but certainly with men on bicycles who want to think they're pretty strong. I suppose it's a lot like drag racing through town to see whose car is the fastest. The classic *mine's bigger than yours* chest pounding thing. Juvenile. Pointless. Indefensible really.

It happens with this young fella and us as we're riding along. And by us, I mean me. We're riding along, accelerating more and more as we ride, pushing each other to see who'll break. Hills are the place where the breaking happens, when one rider or the other can't quite hold the pace up a little hill. This young lion is probably in his 30s, early 40s at the most. He's strong and fit. But there's no doubt about it—he falters on the inclines. Can't keep up with the old man.

Let's hear it for the old guys.

I suspect Dave is oblivious to this. As I've mentioned many times, Dave is always stronger than I am, and *always* makes it up hills faster than I do. This little pissing contest between me and the youngster is most likely completely unnoticed by Dave. Dave's probably just happy that I picked up the pace for a little while.

But the young lion noticed it. And I noticed it. Gloating is such an ugly thing, especially when it stares back at us from the mirror.

Really, let's hear it for the old guys . . .

AN OCEAN, A MOON, AND A SAILBOAT

We shall not cease from exploration
And the end of all our exploring
Will be to arrive where we started
And know the place for the first time.

T.S. Eliot

Light fades into twilight as we move off the streets and onto the paved Baltimore and Annapolis Trail for the final 15 or 20 miles of our day, also the final 15 or 20 miles of our journey across the country. Truly, I feel like I'm high on some sort of drug, sailing down the dusky trail in the cool evening. My elation must be conspicuous to folks around me too, as I end up in conversation with nearly everyone I ride past.

Giddy. That's the word that describes it. Positively giddy. I can rarely remember feeling this way in my life. But it defines both me and the world I'm riding through as I approach this culmination of my journey. I'm fit, strong, healthy and happy. I don't ever want this moment to end.

The trail dumps us onto Highway 450, which I suspect is some form of *old 50*, but my mind is completely consumed with excited anticipation of the upcoming climax of this journey.

It's dark, and our lights flash for the relatively light traffic passing us.

The last few dozen miles have been so flat that it's very noticeable when the road begins to tilt up a bit. I look ahead and see that we're climbing a long bridge. As we climb, I realize that beneath us is the broad mouth of the Severn River, and the bridge is elevated like this to allow tall ships to pass beneath. Not something that landlubbers like myself ever have to think much about.

Dave has dropped back behind to let me lead since I have the magic Garmin. Whenever I'm in front like this, I try to keep a strong and steady pace, because I know that whatever pace I set is going to be something less than Dave would set. Approaching the crest of the bridge, it dawns on me that this bridge takes us across big water and into Annapolis. It takes us across salt water from the Atlantic Ocean.

I haven't really thought about this until this very moment. I've been so consumed with anticipation of the finish that I haven't really thought much about what that finish would look like. Just that it would happen. Right here, at this moment, I'm approaching the crest of the bridge that marks our arrival at our destination.

My mind starts to get this, but my legs just keep turning. They've probably turned the crank of this bicycle a million and a half times on this journey, and climbing this bridge, they just keep doing what they've been doing for 3400 miles. They turn.

Reaching the peak of the span, I look off to my left onto the mouth of the Severn River as it opens into Chesapeake Bay, and my heart and soul take control, turning me and bringing me to the edge of the bridge at its zenith. This is not a moment to miss. Dave is right behind me.

There's a sidewalk at the edge of the road, with a low brick parapet wall and a steel handrail along the top. We lean our bikes against the wall, and rest our arms on the rail as we gaze out to the east over the water below us.

The view out over the Chesapeake takes my breath away.

A lone sailboat drifts south beneath a bright moon rising over the bay.

Gazing out over this beautiful image, I'm mindful of how clumsy words might be right now. But it feels like the shared moment should have shared words. "This is the most beautiful ending to this ride I can imagine," I end up saying.

Dave's looking out across the water as well, and takes his time before answering. His words are slow and deliberate. "It's funny. I was so mad at myself yesterday for not having extra chain links, and all day I've been regretting the late start we got to the day. But without all that, we wouldn't have been here at this moment. This ending is timed perfectly, isn't it?"

"Yeah. The last hour or so riding at dusk along the trail, capped off with this view at the finish line. I don't know how much I believe in the notion that everything happens for a reason, but right now I'm pretty glad that the stars lined up to put us right here, right now."

Then Dave turns toward me with one of the most heartfelt and genuine smiles I've ever seen. He reaches toward me with a handshake, and as I take his hand in warm embrace, he replies with the only word that fits this moment. "Congratulations."

The glint I see could be a little moisture leaking from Dave's eyes, or it could be moist emotion leaking from mine. A moment of shared accomplishment wraps around us, bathed in the glow of the streetlamps that line the bridge, the moonlight bounding off the water below. A million and a half pedal cranks, 3400 miles, 125,000 feet of climbing. It all earned me this moment, and it feels better than I could have imagined.

The lone sailboat out on the bay begins to furl his sails, apparently approaching his destination. Dave and I mount up in silence, and complete the final pedal strokes down to the Annapolis waterfront. We follow the Garmin through the dark streets of Annapolis to our hotel, feeling a chill as the air cools for the evening. But that's just on the outside.

EPILOGUE

Come grow old with me. The best is yet to be.
William Wordsworth

Dave and I checked into our room at the Marriott in downtown Annapolis, then walked across the Compromise Bridge, and had dinner at the Boatyard Bar and Grill. Maryland crab cakes of course, along with a couple of longnecks. We were wrapped in a sense of shared accomplishment, something beyond words, really. What can be said at a time like that?

We'd completed something very big for both of us, and it felt good. I reflected on the time and effort spent in making the trip happen. We spend our lives investing in the things that become our life, building equity in ourselves and those around us. In the end, if there's some sort of surprise pop quiz we take on our way out, will we be happy with the results of our decisions? We give our lives to become who we are, and at some point we need to ask whether we're worth what we paid.

Sitting with Dave, the dearest of friends to me, sharing a beer and basking in the quiet that only the best of friends can share, I realized that this journey was, indeed, a good investment. It made me a better me. At the same time, while we lounged in the warmth of achievement, I found myself looking forward more than backward, looking toward the next thing. It bothered me a bit, and I think Dave might have been feeling the same thing.

It wasn't anti-climactic so much as post-climactic. The climax really occurred as we crossed the bridge and gazed out across the mouth of the Severn River emptying into Chesapeake Bay, a sailboat crossing the mouth beneath a dazzling moon that was just a couple of days from full. For me, that was the point of completion. After that, it was just wrapping up and looking forward.

Funny that I felt guilt over this. I remember the niggling feeling inside myself that I should feel more festivity after the completion of the ride, shouldn't I? I should be jubilant, and the moment of celebration should be upon me, right?

I felt good. I felt strong. I felt a deep sense of satisfaction. I felt immensely happy and contented as Dave and I shared our celebratory dinner and beer.

But I was looking forward. The warmth of accomplishment was shining on my back, while my face looked toward the next thing.

Big moments are like that in life. They happen, then they're past. No matter how much we try to orchestrate the moments that we want to remember, the ones we remember are the ones that catch us a little off guard. Then they're past. Try to recreate or improve them, and the real value in the moment starts to drift away.

The moon hanging above that sailboat in the bay was in the perfect place that evening as we crossed the bridge. A day later and it would have been too low on the horizon, a day earlier and it would have been too high in the sky. That morning was the only time on the entire journey across the country where we weren't pedaling before daybreak, thanks to a mechanical problem, and if it weren't for that mechanical problem, we would never have been on that bridge at just the right time to be part of that scene.

I didn't plan the mechanical problem, or the time of day, or the phase of the moon. That's just the way things came together, and my heart recognized the moment. I didn't keep pedaling across the bridge, taking casual notice of the scene over my left shoulder, but instead listened to the song of a moment that called to me. My soul recognized it for the moment of climax that it was, bringing tears of joy to my eyes as I basked in the moment.

Then it was over, and everything except my brain realized that the moment on the bridge had been the point of celebration, and that the moment was past. My poor little brain couldn't figure out why I was feeling guilty about not wanting to pour champagne all over everything. So I just basked in the quiet goodness, and shared a moment of deep and abiding friendship with Dave.

I spent sunrise the next morning standing on the Compromise Bridge, looking down at the sailboats in the yacht basin, wondering if any of them had been the one we'd seen the night before. I rented a car, and Dave and I spent the morning getting our bikes packed up for shipping, then dropped them off at FedEx. After dropping Dave off at National Airport, I drove out toward the mountains, where I dropped my rental car off and made my way to a little house in a little town in the foothills of the Shenandoah.

I sat on the porch and waited for the woman who lived there to get home. She was a teacher at a little country school there in the foothills, and we had some unfinished business.

Long ago, we knew each other well enough to feel ourselves falling for one another. We spent one afternoon together, exploring the Flint Hills of Kansas on the back of a motorcycle, feeling the depth of something that scared us both.

A moment. One that caught us both off guard. One that neither of us was ready for. A moment that we embraced, then let slip through our fingers, each of us with a different orchestration of life that we were pursuing. For over 35 years, we'd known nothing of each other, and buried deeper and deeper beneath life was the memory we both carried of that day.

Like a seed, laying dormant beneath life. A seed that, in most cases, would never have germinated. But in our case, some series of odd quirks and starts and stops brought us both to this funny moment, at the end of my bike ride, after two 30-year marriages had ended.

Her name was Christine.

I stood on the porch of her 200-year-old house, on the edge of the woods, along the threshold of the Shenandoah, and watched a car pull into her driveway. She stepped out of the car, leaned against it, and smiled at me. I remembered that smile, though it now had a bit more wisdom and a little less innocence behind it. I smiled back, and recognized instantly a thing I'd felt many decades ago. A seed, left slumbering, suddenly and unexpectedly awake.

We walked toward each other, maybe a bit like we once walked toward each other on the tennis court. The ball rested on the ground there. It had been there a long time, waiting for us to come back to it and finish the game we'd started. She sparkled with something I could feel, a resonance that hummed in me. A bit like that Martin felt resonating against me back in Missouri, on that evening when I didn't have the courage to play.

I reached out toward Christine as she came close, wondering what sort of hug we'd have for each other. She came into my arms, and we held each other, feeling the resonance that came from somewhere in the touch.

Earlier in my journey, I'd admonished myself for failing to have the courage to coax music from a beautiful old Martin that I stumbled onto. A regret for a thing not done, music not played, a chance to explore ignored. The resonance against me in the touch of Christine felt very similar. A graceful bloom of harmony, deep and beautiful, come to rest in my arms.

When the Universe drops something like that in front of us, we need to pick it up and play.

A wonderful quote from Rumi goes something like this:

Lovers don't finally meet somewhere. They're in each other all along.

Maybe that's true, maybe it's not. I'm no expert on love. I know that standing in the shade in front of that old house, the notion of starting up a love affair wasn't high on my to-do list, and I suspect it wasn't for Christine either. At 60 years old, life had become simple for both of us, and the complexity of a long distance relationship wasn't part of the orchestration.

And yet . . .

Nearly four decades ago I had seen something pretty over my shoulder, but hadn't stopped to fall into the moment. This time, I did more than glance over my shoulder. I listened to the song of the moment singing to me. A little sooner wouldn't have worked, a little later probably wouldn't have, either. Life had worked the necessary delays into the timeline so I'd be at the right place at the right time.

At that moment,
> standing on the porch of the old house,
>> seeing Christine leaning against her car,
>>> the moon was just right.

I heard the whisper of a place calling to me,
> and let myself fall into it,
>> and it into me.

ACKNOWLEDGMENTS

Gratitude is the wine for the soul.
Go on. Get Drunk.

Rumi

Lots of folks helped me put this book together or leant me a hand with permissions or advice, and for all of that help I'm very grateful. There are a couple of people in particular I'd like to acknowledge.

Dave Giesler is a true and great friend, and the best long-distance riding companion on earth. As I was writing the early drafts of this book, Dave was an excellent sounding board and a good advisor for style, strategy and content. Not to mention that he kept me in check regarding the relative accuracy of my narrative. Thanks for your friendship, Dave; thanks for all your help making this book happen, and thanks for being such a good sport when I poke fun at us.

Chris Feld and Michele Lloyd were important beta readers for me. They provided valuable advice and excellent input, and helped me to craft a better story. Thanks, Chris and Michele.

Thanks to Jim Hoy for allowing me to reprint material

from his book *Flint Hills Cowboys,* and for his expertise and guidance regarding the Flint Hills region.

Thanks to Aaron Brachfeld for acting as a consultant for me on farming and ranching techniques in the Great Plains.

My children are voracious readers yet they rarely read my books, so they'll likely not see this and be embarrassed by it. But just in case, thank you Jesse, Ian, and Anna for being such wonderful human beings. You each continue to be a wellspring of joy and delight in my life.

Christine is a gem in my life that was tucked away and hidden many years ago. Pure and simple luck brought us together again after nearly four decades. I'm privileged and delighted to dance together again in the late summer prairie. Thanks, Christine, for letting me tell a little bit of our story in this book.

Your acts of kindness are iridescent wings.
Rumi

WHAT DID YOU THINK?

Review this book on Amazon.
> https://www.amazon.com/dp/B01DWPRW5U

Review this book on Goodreads.
> https://www.goodreads.com/book/show/
> 30175051-pilgrim-spokes

I'd would love your feedback directly:
> NeilHansonAuthor@gmail.com

Buy *Pilgrim Wheels*—The first part of the journey story based on my cross-country trip, from Monterey on the west coast to Medicine Lodge in Kansas.
> https://www.amazon.com/dp/B00SXIK9WK

Buy *The Pilgrim Way*— A complete description of the logistics, route, and details of my journey across America; an essential guide for those considering long-distance touring in general, or a cross-country trek specifically.
> https://www.amazon.com/dp/B00SP5WM7Q

ABOUT THE AUTHOR

A lifelong cyclist, Neil Hanson's two-wheeled adventures have taken him across America, along the Natchez Trace, and throughout northern Italy. Originally from Kansas, Neil currently lives in Colorado, where he navigates his bicycle up and down the inclines of the Rocky Mountains. His books include *Pilgrim Wheels*, part one of the deep and introspective journey story woven around his cross-country trip that concludes in *Pilgrim Spokes*, as well as a how-to minimalist-touring guide, *The Pilgrim Way*.

READING GROUP QUESTIONS

If your book club is reading *Pilgrim Spokes*, or if you're considering it as a book club selection, here are some possible questions to spark conversation.

1. A recurring theme in the book is the notion of regrets and how we deal with them in life. In a couple of different places the author talks about people who say they have no regrets in life, and that he doesn't believe that's possible. How do people in the group feel about regrets?

2. Sticking with the regrets theme, when the author has lunch with Ann in Greencastle, they talk a lot about the notion of regrets, and fit it into a context where they invent the phrase "shuddering gremlins." How does this perspective that they arrived at differ from your perspective?

3. The author reflects in a couple places on what he believes is a typical pattern in marriage relationships, referring to the possibility that in our lives, we may need "three marriages." He refines that with the belief that if things go well, all three marriages can be within a single marriage, as we evolve into each of the relationship types with the same person. Does this fit with what you've observed in your life?

4. Did the author's description of his passionate enjoyment of hunting resonate with any passion you have in your own life as it relates to an activity or a pursuit? Did his perspective change your perspective toward hunting in any way?

5. The author describes the places he travels through in a way that makes it easy to feel like you're there with him. Did any of those descriptions alter your perception of the place at all? For example, people often think of Kansas as a big flat state, but the couple days of riding he did in the Flint Hills described beautiful rolling hills in a way that people don't often associate with Kansas.

6. Which character that the author meets on his journey do you most identify with, and why?

7. What was your reaction to the author's discussion of class and aristocracy when he stayed in the Butler's Quarters in the mansion along the Mississippi river?

8. Do you agree with the author's assertion that comfort is largely defined by discomfort, and that sometimes misery is an important element in true and deep enjoyment of a simple thing. His example of enjoying a warm shower and bed after a miserable, cold, and wet day of riding was the context for that discussion, and he used the example of his adventure in the Ozark Mountains with his brother years ago in the freezing rain, culminating in a bowl of warm chili, as further example.

9. When the author met his old friend Cathy for dinner in Indianapolis, he was surprised by her anger over his divorce. On reflection he came to see her anger within the context of a thing he referred to as "tribal equity" that comes to be manifested in a think like marriage. In what ways do the author's ideas resonate with you, and in what ways do you disagree?

10. When the author talked about his bad decision to stay on US 40 in Pennsylvania rather than riding on the GAP trail as originally planned, did the process of falling into the bad decision resonate with you in any way?

11. In the final chapter of the book, the author describes a euphoric feeling of accomplishment as he and Dave crossed the bridge into Annapolis. Did this description bring to mind an event or time in your life when you felt a similar powerful sense?

12. In the epilogue, the author describes meeting Christine again after many years, then he leaves us hanging with regard to whether or not their relationship blossomed into anything. What do you think the odds are for and against "rediscovered" relationships, and what do you guess happened with the author and Christine?

13. We all look for adventure in different ways in our lives. For the author, adventure was defined as riding his bicycle across the country, half of the time by himself. This put him at a increased risk. Does adventure always bring increased risk with it? How does our assessment of potential risk help us define our appetite for adventure? What are the other factors that help us each define the adventures we want to pursue in life?

MORE BY NEIL M. HANSON

Most of what Neil writes falls into the Creative Nonfiction category, just like this one. He likes to call it the Art of Truth It's reflective storytelling; searching for insight, wrestling with experience for wisdom and perspective.

CYCLING REFLECTIONS

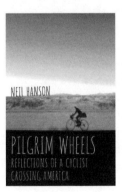

BOOK ONE: *Pilgrim Wheels* (2015) — A deep exploration of the western half of Neil's bicycle journey across America, beginning in Monterey, CA and concluding in Medicine Lodge, KS. This is a book for those who enjoy thoughtful and reflective storytelling, focused on the experience of the journey more than the details of the ride. (For the "how-to" description of the bicycle ride, see *The Pilgrim Way* below.)

https://www.amazon.com/dp/
B00SXIK9WK

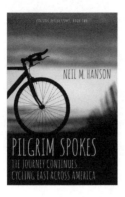

BOOK TWO: *Pilgrim Spokes* (2016) — A deep exploration of the eastern half of Neil's bicycle journey across America, beginning in Medicine Lodge, KS and concluding in Annapolis, MD. A book for those who enjoy thoughtful and reflective storytelling, as well as a deeply personal tale of transition.

https://www.amazon.com/dp/ B01DWPRW5U

BOOK THREE: *Pilgriming the Trace* (Scheduled for 2017) — Neil and Dave continue their sojourning, this time on the Natchez Trace and joined by Neil's son Ian. From Baton Rouge to Nashville, Neil explores what can only be described as a national treasure for the cyclist.

OTHER CYCLING BOOKS

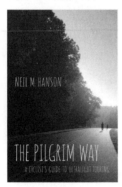

The Pilgrim Way (2015) — This is the book for those how are looking for a turn by turn description of the logistics, route, and details of Neil's journey across America. It's an essential guide for those considering long-distance touring in general, or a cross-country trek specifically. If you want a "how-to" description of ultralight bicycle touring in general, and a cross-country route specifically, this is the book for you, with images added in the print edition.

https://www.amazon.com/dp/ B00SP5WM7Q

NON-CYCLING BOOKS

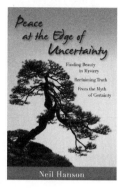

Peace at the Edge of Uncertainty (2010) — Neil's first book is a spiritual story of transition woven around the final days and hours that he shares with his dying father, and the mystical events that are part of that experience.

https://www.amazon.com/dp/ B003N3V01E